D1380491

A DRIVE ON THE
Wild SIDE
Alistair Weaver

First published in September 2007 by Veloce Publishing Limited, 33 Trinity Street, Dorchester DT1 1TT, England. Fax 01305 268864/e-mail info@veloce.co.uk/web www.veloce.co.uk or www.velocebooks.com.
ISBN: 978-1-845841-00-3/UPC: 6-36847-04100-7

British Library Cataloguing in Publication Data - A catalogue record for this book is available from the British Library. Typesetting, design and page make-up all by Veloce Publishing Ltd on Apple Mac.
Printed in India by Replika Press.

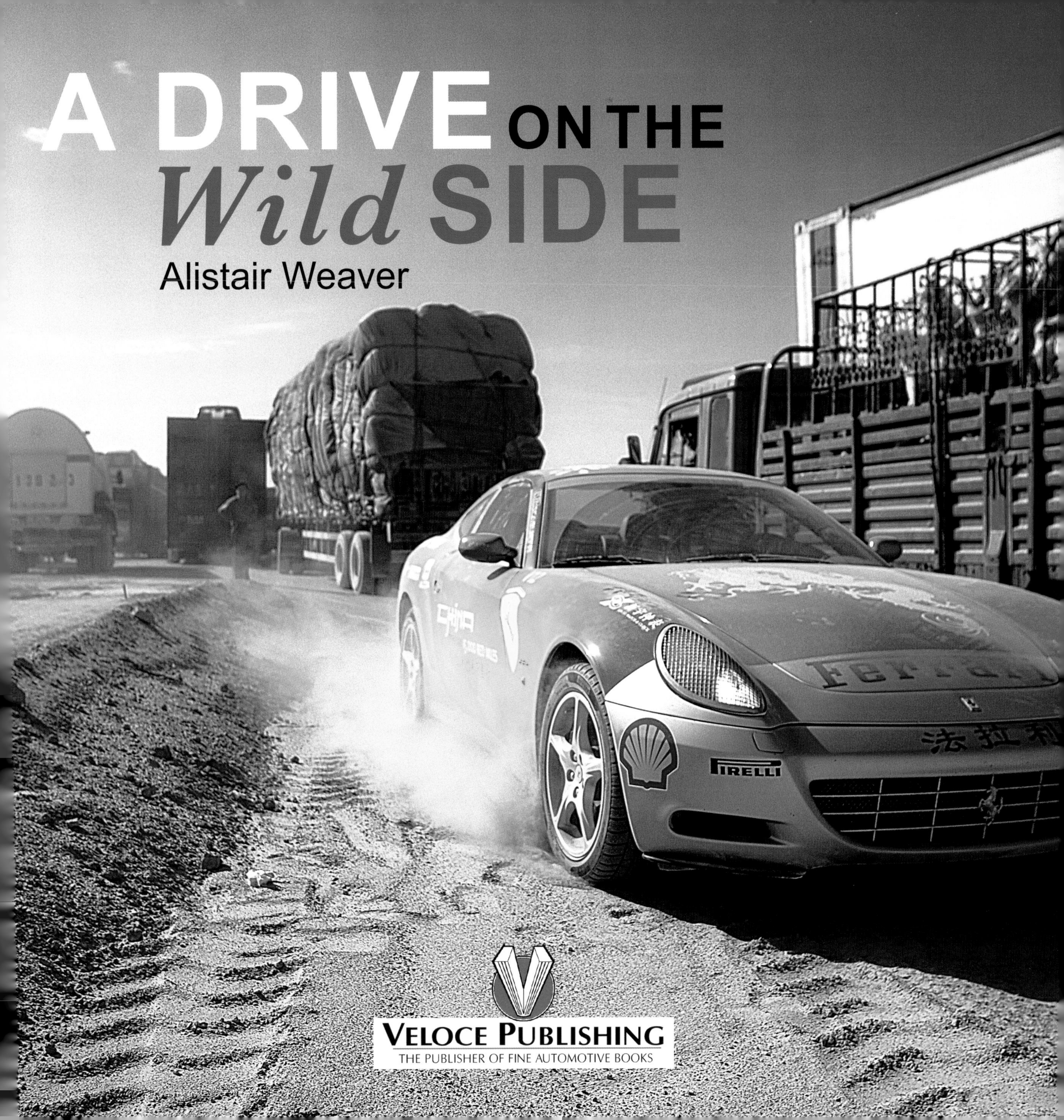
A DRIVE ON THE
Wild SIDE
Alistair Weaver
PIRELLI
VELOCE PUBLISHING
THE PUBLISHER OF FINE AUTOMOTIVE BOOKS

CONTENTS

ACKNOWLEDGEMENTS

It almost goes without saying that none of these stories would have been possible without the help and support of a huge range of people. Thanks are due, for example, to the legion of press officers who not only listened to my crazy ideas but helped me realise them. "So, Alistair, you want to take a ForTwo to the Arctic?" said Debbie Hull, the PR Manager of Smart in the UK. "Great idea, let me see what I can do."

My gratitude should also go to the photographers who not only created some stunning images, but also endured several days in a car with me and my eclectic taste in music. "So, you want to take a £35k X3, £20k worth of camera gear and me into Soweto?" said Waldo van der Waal. "OK, I'll help organise the car."

Publisher Rod Grainger and designer Stacey Grove have shown remarkable tolerance and good humour in the face of an author with strong opinions. Both have contributed hugely to this book. I am also grateful to the publications – *4Car, Autocar, Edmunds' Inside Line, European Car, Motor Trend, Octane, Sunday Times* and *Top Gear* – which gave me permission to reproduce the text as it appeared in their pages.

Thanks must go to my parents who bought me my first car magazine when I was ten, and then had to listen as I recited all manner of dull statistics about power and performance. My girlfriend, Amanda, deserves immense credit for putting up with a boyfriend who's often on the other side of the world when he should be cooking dinner in London. Too often, I've crawled home tired and tetchy from the latest adventure.

To all those who have made this possible, thank you.

Alistair Weaver

INTRODUCTION

From time to time I'm asked to appear on television to debate a motoring topic. I'll normally be pitched against an environmental campaigner who views motoring journalists as the spawn of Satan. We'll be asked to wait our turn together, like two boxers sharing the same dressing room. Often, the exchanges that take place off camera are the most interesting.

In January 2007, I found myself waiting outside a BBC studio with Cllr Jenny Jones AM, a member of the British Green Party. The subject of air travel and its environmental impact was dominating the news agenda and I admitted that I spend much of my life in a 'plane.

"I accept there's a problem," I said, "but I'm concerned that without travel, we would have less tolerance and understanding of other peoples and cultures." The Councillor eyed me suspiciously. "That's rubbish," she retorted. "Travel breeds intolerance because people take their culture with them."

It was a staggering statement and one with which I could not possibly agree. Although the modern news media has brought the world to our living room, it focuses on triumph or despair, scandal and outrage. If a place is no longer newsworthy, it is no longer on the news.

Travel allows you to look beyond the headlines. The cosmopolitan Beirut I discovered was very different to the war zone I remembered from the news. Likewise, the social deprivation of western China was far removed from the contemporary image of a tiger economy. Even the US can seem a very different place to that portrayed by Hollywood or CNN.

Seeing things for yourself can make you reassess your own values and opinions. On Africa's Masai Steppe, I witnessed a celebration of female circumcision. It did not make me feel any easier about this awful practice, but it did give me a fascinating insight into a human society with a very different view of life.

I have been exceptionally fortunate to be able to combine my love of travel with my love of cars. Even in my early childhood I had a passion for all things automotive and, by the age of ten, I could recite the 0-60mph time of every car on sale. I determined to make cars my career and, aged just 21, I was lucky enough to become a roadtester at *Autocar* magazine.

In the past decade, I've driven almost every car on sale, often in fascinating locations. This book is a compendium of some of my favourite drives from across the world. In each case, I've tried to put you, the reader, in the driver's seat and to describe the emotion of the journey. I hope that I've succeeded and that you enjoy the ride.

ENGINE START
Ferrari

FERRARI TO CHINA

An epic drive along China's Silk Road in Maranello's finest

Photographs ANTON WATTS

It's not everyday that you get asked this question: 'Would you like to go to China to drive a leg of Ferrari's 15,000 Red Miles?' To my mind it was a rhetorical question: the trip combined two irresistible ingredients – the Far East and a Ferrari. I was packing before the conversation had finished.

As a motoring journalist, you are paid for your impartiality. As one of Europe's more celebrated scribes once put it, "Every car is a shitbox until proven otherwise". This dictum must remain true, but it is equally true that to do this job properly, you have to be a car nut. And it is very difficult indeed to be a car nut without having a passion for Ferrari.

While my adolescent contemporaries were busy discussing the curves of Erika Eleniak or Pamela Anderson, I would be lusting after the latest product of Maranello. Cars such as the F40 and the Testarossa defined my childhood as clearly as my first snog (thank you Tracy) or my first pint of beer.

I can always remember the first time I drove a Ferrari. It was during my time as an Autocar roadtester and I'd just turned twenty-two. One damp summer's evening, I was left alone at a UK test facility and charged with recording performance figures for the new 360 Modena. Peering down at the yellow Prancing Horse badge on the steering wheel, it was difficult not to be emotional.

Several years later, the chance to drive a Ferrari in China sounded like a Boy's Own adventure, but I still had a couple of misgivings. From the outset I was certain that I wanted to take part in one of the extreme legs. To make the story work, I needed a genuine adventure – there wasn't much of a story in driving a Ferrari around the highly developed streets of Shanghai. As it turned out, the leg from Kashgar to Jiayuguan couldn't have been more interesting. This was the Wild West, Chinese-style.

My other misgiving concerned the nature of the trip. I had been working on an idea to take a Ferrari to the Great Wall of China for a couple of years but, in the end, the factory beat me to it. There could be no disguising that this was a marketing exercise designed to generate media exposure for a company that doesn't advertise, and to introduce the brand to China.

Normally when I travel, I like to act spontaneously, to get lost in a bid to discover the unexpected. At most there will be three people in the team: myself, a photographer and, on occasion, a local guide. But on this trip, I would be part of a convoy, with little opportunity to do my own thing.

This also turned out to be less of a concern than I'd imagined. At times, the size of our convoy made me feel claustrophobic and there were arguments, but such was the wealth of our experiences that it never became a big problem. On this occasion, the story came to me.

PetroChina
中国石油

Manpower is the driving force of China's economic renaissance; concentration is everything on dusty, dangerous roads

This is not a good start. Night has fallen in Kashi and our old Volkswagen taxi has broken down. We stand by the roadside and watch our driver stare at the engine in a fit of desperation. I can't remember the Chinese words for "alternator broken," so we hail another cab as he waits for a tow.

Kashi lies on the western tip of China, about 2000 miles due west of Beijing and less than 200 miles from the border with Afghanistan. Officially, this area is called the Xinjiang Uighur Autonomous Region, and it's a world away from my perceived image of China. Islam, not communism, is the dominant belief system here, and you're more likely to be served a mutton kebab than Beijing Duck.

The people don't look or sound Chinese, and few have ever heard the word Ferrari. Even a bicycle is beyond the means of most residents, which makes the presence outside our hotel of two 612 Scagliettis seem even more incongruous. Unlikely though it might sound, these cars will be my friends and guides for the next five days as I drive 1800 miles along the Silk Road, the old trading route between East and West. In other words, I will pilot a $247,850 supercar where Marco Polo once rode.

For me, this is a mighty step into the unknown, but for the cars and their support staff, this is just another leg in an epic journey that began in Beijing on August 29. By the time they reach the finish line in Shanghai on October 29, the cars will have covered more than 15,000 miles. Part PR stunt and part durability test, the 15,000 Red Miles is the most ambitious trip ever undertaken by the folks from Maranello.

Today's stage starts at 8:30am, when it's still dark. Despite being geographically closer to Europe than it is to the Chinese capital, Xinjiang still adheres to Beijing time. Its residents therefore live in a bizarre world wherein it doesn't get light until mid-morning and then stays light late into the evening.

We tack southeast, picking a route along the edge of the Tarim Basin and in the shadow of the Kunlun Shan mountains. Dusty desert wastelands are interspersed by tiny oases of paddy and cotton fields. China is home to 1.3 billion people, but few of them live out here.

The view beyond the Ferrari's fluted hood is far removed from the high-rise, first-world extravagance of contemporary Shanghai, but there are still signs of China's rapid economic growth. Mobile phone towers are dotted across the horizon, and the buzz of my cell phone provides a link, literally and metaphorically, to the developed world.

The roads are surprisingly good, and we settle to an easy, 80mph cruise. The

Punctures are an occupational hazard on the rock strewn roads; getting a temporary driving licence was probably the trip's biggest challenge

612 is billed as the consummate GT, with enough room in the back for a couple of slimline adults and a refined, relaxed gait. In sixth gear, with the big V12 barely ticking over, the Ferrari is as quiet as an executive sedan, and the suspension revisions have done little to compromise its comfortable ride. The 612 is a subtle, sophisticated tool – it's happy to leave the pornstar antics to the F430.

Ferrari's 15,000 Red Miles is the brainchild of aftersales director Luigino "Gigi" Barp. "This is the first time any manufacturer has attempted such a feat in China," he says. "By describing the tour as a sporting event, we gained the permission of Chinese authorities, without which it would've been impossible." A government official has joined the team for the duration, doubling as a tour guide.

The logistical challenge shouldn't be underestimated. Just to secure a temporary driving permit for China, I had to submit a copy of my résumé and eight photographs to the highest authorities. There could be no flexibility; an Italianate laissez-faire attitude wasn't going to work.

The Ferrari caravan consists of seven full-time support staff, which includes two engineers and a truckful of spares. We are the red squadron," says Barp, a former member of the Italian air force. "We have clear rules and strict discipline. People must know and trust the boss – me."

A Fiat hatchback performs a reconnaissance role, relaying information about the road ahead. Its importance is demonstrated on day one, when the newly laid highway momentarily ceases to be. We're diverted off-road onto a rough gravel track that would trouble an SUV. The closest most Ferrari drivers come to such conditions is a pebble-driveway.

The quality of the roads isn't nearly as bad as the quality of the driving. The highways aren't so much roads as tarmac strips upon which the locals see fit to travel. Officially, you drive on the right in China, but no one seems to care. It's not unusual to find a horse and cart trundling toward you on the wrong side of the road; motorbikes scurry every which way, and no one stops at an intersection.

At first, it looks like organized chaos, but it's not long before I pass a truck that's rolled off the road. With car sales rising 30 per cent in 2005 to 3.2 million, road safety is becoming a major concern for the Chinese government. In the Tarim Basin, there's no emergency room, and no one will hear you scream.

By the end of the second day, we've arrived in the small town of Minfeng, on the edge of the Taklimakan Desert. The town has a main street, which is littered with tiny cafés and stalls. In the center of the street, a local butcher wheels a still-warm carcass of mutton past busy shoppers; there's no refrigeration, so the meat must be sold fresh.

法拉利

612 SCAGLIETTI
新宇钟表
12
CHINA
FERRARI 15.000 RED MILES
法拉利红色万里行

Ferrari
法拉利
PIRELLI

'I'm cruising through a Chinese desert in a Ferrari at near three-figure speeds, with my iPod singing sweet tunes and the air-conditioning maintaining a steady 70 degrees. I've been on fairground rides that felt less surreal.'

I park the Ferrari, and it immediately draws a crowd. The locals peer through the windows and grab aggressively at the door handles. Through a translator, I snatch a word with a bystander named Uquili. He claims to have seen a Grand Prix on television, but has no knowledge of Ferrari's road cars. "I have no money," he says,"but I am confident that in the future I will afford a car."

His words appease concerns about the ethics of driving such a conspicuous symbol of wealth through such a poor area. Although Ferrari expects to sell around 140 cars in China this year, they'll be sold to Shanghai entrepreneurs, not cotton farmers from Minfeng. Ferrari's PR guru, Antonio Ghini, is dismissive of such criticism: "Italy was poor in the postwar period," he says, "but a Ferrari was a stimulating message, an inspiration. I believe it can play the same role in China today."

Next morning, we leave Minfeng and head due north, bisecting the desert. Covering an area of more than 127,000 square miles, the Taklimakan is the second largest desert in the world. The locals call it the "sea of death," and it's easy to see why. While the natural beauty of the dunes is undeniable, it's difficult to think of a more inhospitable environment.

The anonymity of the sand is broken only by the occasional camel train and a sprinkling of homes that derive their subsistence from God knows where. Only after 120 miles are we afforded some relief in the form of the desert's only fuel station. Its name, appropriately, is Midpoint.

This is a strange sort of a day. I'm cruising through a Chinese desert in a Ferrari at near three-figure speeds, with my iPod singing sweet tunes and the air-conditioning maintaining a steady 70 degrees. I've been on fairground rides that felt less surreal.

Our speeds are relatively modest, but there are still times when I can't resist slipping down a couple of cogs and asking the 5.7-litre V12 to draw breath. On this fuel, the engine is delivering significantly less than the claimed 540 horsepower and 434 poundfeet of torque, but the 612 should still be described as pleasingly rapid. The V12 is so quiet – too quiet for my liking – and so unerringly smooth that this car gathers speed by stealth.

I've spent time over the past couple of days swapping between the silver car, which boasts a manual trans, and the red car, which has a semi-automatic F1 gearbox. By day three, I've surprised myself by preferring the F1. These systems have improved dramatically in recent years, and on long journeys such as this, it's ultimately the more relaxing and fulfilling companion.

There's much to like about Ferrari's most grown up car, but it's not without fault. The faux-aluminum switchgear, aftermarket stereo, and tacky CD holders, for example, compromise what's otherwise a beautifully finished cabin. To these eyes, at least, the 612's styling also continues to frustrate; the "Scaglietti scallops" look especially contrived.

It's mid-afternoon by the time we reach the northern edge of the desert, where we discover its hidden treasure. A Sinopec installation sucks oil from the desert floor, driving China's economic renaissance. A makeshift village has sprung up to service the workforce, and as we head east toward my final destination of Jiayuguan, we encounter more nomadic communities, serving the railroad or highway construction.

Groups of workers labor around the clock to transform the arid landscape, and the pace of change is extraordinary. This route, which in medieval times witnessed the trade of iron, silk, china, fruit, and gems, will once again buzz with the sound of commerce. In a few months' time, the main highway will be complete, but for now we're forced to drive for more than 120 miles on rutted dirt roads that cause the whole car to shake in anger.

In near zero visibility, we push on, relying on our reflexes and the strength of the 612's suspension. The Prancing Horse on the steering wheel bucks uneasily in my hands as we play chicken with the overloaded trucks that prowl the highway. There's little time for reflection; the clock is ticking and the thought of tackling

'The Great Wall is arguably the most potent symbol of ancient China, but with its manicured car parks and garish tourists, it's also an emblem of the new China.'

such terrain in the dark is nothing short of terrifying.

The road finally improves as the city of Jiayuguan looms large on the horizon. We're now in the Gansu province, beyond the Tarim Basin and in a much more affluent area. Historically referred to as the mouth of China, it holds a symbolic location at the end of the Great Wall.

On our final morning, the Ferrari and I pay homage to one of man's greatest feats. The Great Wall is arguably the most potent symbol of ancient China, but with its manicured car parks and garish tourists, it's also an emblem of the new China. It seems as good a place as any to wave goodbye to the red squadron.

The cynics will dismiss Ferrari's 15,000 Red Miles as nothing more than a PR stunt from a company that doesn't advertise. But while they're correct about the motive, they underestimate the triumph of the execution. Anyone who dodged the Beijing traffic, scaled the Tibetan peaks, or crossed the Taklimakan Desert will have been left in no doubt that this was an epic journey.

First printed in Motor Trend magazine, April 2006

Ferrari
法拉利
PIRELLI
PIRELLI
CHINA
15,000 RED MILES

NISSAN TO MOUNT FUJI

A drive from Tokyo to the top of Mount Fuji

Photographs LEE BRIMBLE

Some of the toilets in Japan are a work of genius. First, the toilet seat rotates through a cleaning mechanism to reveal a sanitised throne. Next, it is heated to a user-selected temperature. Then, when one has done one's business, a small jet motors forth from the back of the bowl to squirt one's nether regions, which is a surprisingly satisfying experience. Some of the more compact models even have the washbasin built into the top of the cistern – when you press the flush button, it automatically activates the tap. Brilliant.

For me, these sanitary wonders epitomise much of what is right about modern Japan. This is a culture with a passion for detail that is not afraid to apply new thinking to age-old problems. In Japan, you dry your hands using a blower that faces up so that any drips are caught in the tray below. In the West, such machines blow down so any drips fall on the floor or your clothes. It's a small detail, but it makes a big difference.

I've been to Tokyo many times, for motor shows, technical seminars and such-like, but I cannot claim to 'know' Tokyo as I do New York or Sydney. To western eyes emerging from a 12-hour flight, it always seems a baffling maze of high-rise buildings and neon signs.

In most cities, it's possible to identify one area from another – Clapham in London is architecturally very different from Knightsbridge, for example – but in Tokyo everything seems to merge into one. Such is the Japanese passion for modernity that there is very little of what you might call classical architecture. Everything looks like it has been built since 1960.

But I'd always suspected that life outside Tokyo would be rather different. Friends who had lived in the Far East during their university gap years told of towns in which no-one spoke English, and in which a white westerner was regarded as a curiosity.

A plan was hatched to drive from Ginza, the commercial heart of modern Tokyo, to the top of Mount Fuji. This would give me at least a taste of the Japan beyond the skyscrapers. I was also excited by the opportunity to stay in a Ryokan, which offers a more traditional alternative to Tokyo's generic, business hotels.

The Ryokan experience was memorable for many things. The food and the bath you can read about overleaf, but one anecdote failed to make the cut. During the meal we were asked if we would like a post-dinner massage and purely in the interests of journalistic integrity, photographer Lee and I agreed.

More often than not in the Far East, the masseuse is a pretty young girl, skilled in the art of manipulation. After a couple of beers, Lee and I had high hopes for this experience. But when the doors opened the masseuses turned out to be 70 year-old ladies, who found themselves confronted by two western men wearing boxer shorts and a dressing gown. It was difficult to know who was more shocked, them or us.

横浜335
な・3 50

The underground car park at Nissan's HQ in Tokyo is like a secret toy shop. Here, in these dimly lit bays, you will find all manner of strange vehicles, some of which are destined for these shores, and others that will never escape the land of the rising sun. Today, a diminutive and oh-so-cool Cube shares a bay with an executive Fuga, while the tedious Tiida MPV holds a watching brief.

The car I'm here to drive sits in another corner. We've already driven the 350Z Roadster in the US but the UK version won't arrive until March. Based on the much-admired 350Z Coupé, the Roadster will cost from £26,000, some £1500 more than the hardtop. It'll be mine for the next couple of days, during which time I'll flee the clutches of Tokyo in search of a traditional Japanese Ryokan hotel, before scampering up the slopes of the famous Mount Fuji. It should be quite a trip.

Tokyo is a far less daunting city in which to drive than most European capitals. The 8.1 million workaholics who call it home live ordered, conservative lives and this is reflected in their driving. The traffic is no worse than London's and everything moves along in neat columns. And because almost everyone uses high-tech satellite navigation systems, there is none of the desperado lane-swapping that makes Madrid or Milan such a challenge.

But while Tokyo is ordered, it could never be described as beautiful. Although the preponderance of Japanese characters in bright neon lends it a distinct flavour, it has little genuine character. Most of the buildings are new and high-rise, while the only interesting modern architecture appears to have been commissioned by the European fashion emporiums such as Louis Vuitton.

Most western visitors never leave the capital city, which is a shame because visitors to Tokyo gain only a one-dimensional view of Japan. No sooner have we left the city limits on the Tomei Expressway than the scenery shifts and the horizon is dominated by the looming presence of Mount Fuji. At 3776m high, Fuji rivals Vesuvius for the title of best-known volcano. It's still active, but the last time it spat forth was in 1707 and the last large eruption was as long ago as 930BC. No worries today, then.

The motorway slog offers me a chance to gather my first impressions of the car. The transition from hard to soft-top has done little to compromise the Z's appearance. At the tug of a handle and the flick of a switch the roof disappears behind a solid cover in a mere 20 seconds to leave a chunky, dramatic profile. To these eyes it looks terrific – purposeful yet authentic.

Fears that the drop-top would shake like a teen on a first date can also be allayed. Structural reinforcements have added 53kg to the car's mass but succeeded in creating a car that feels impressively stiff, at least when allied to the softer suspension set-up fitted to Japanese models. The addition of a subtle glass wind deflector behind the rear seats has also created a cabin that's pleasingly free of wind buffeting, even at motorway speeds.

After about sixty miles, we dive off the highway and pick up the Hakone Skyline Driveway which, as its name suggests, leads to the tourist-trap town of Hakone. These roads are used by Japanese journos to test new cars, and it's not difficult to see why. A challenging series of switchbacks that wind their way up hill are a test of man and machine.

The softer suspension settings deny the Roadster the rapier-like responses of the European-spec coupé, but the linear, talkative steering remains. By using the brakes to transfer the weight to the nose, it's possible to quell the initial understeer and encourage the car to bite hard into the turn. This technique works well but my reward is a soft brake pedal and some smoking front discs. One suspects that the brake's specification will need to be upgraded for Europe.

We're to spend the night in the Mikawaya Ryokan hotel, which has been entertaining guests since 1883. Arriving a little before 5pm, photographer Brimble and I are escorted to our rooms by a serious-looking Japanese maid named Misawa. In broken English, she explains that we must change into our

'Tokyo is a far less daunting city in which to drive than most European capitals.'

HAKONE SKYLINE
一旦停止

'We finally emerge above the cloud-line to be greeted by the snowy peak of the volcano. This is the Fuji that you see on postcards.'

Yukata – a kind of cotton dressing gown – and prepare for our bath. Dinner will be served promptly at 7:30pm.

Bathing in a Ryokan follows a strict etiquette and is not for the self-conscious. In a communal but single-sex bath, you strip naked, rinse, and then plunge in the searing heat of natural spring water. Next, you hop out, perch on a tiny stool – awkward for a chap, indecent for a girl – wash, rinse and then return to the pool. It's an elaborate, time-consuming and sometimes awkward process but we emerge feeling fantastic.

We return to find Misawa already serving dinner in our private dining room. Don't be fooled by the taste of sushi in your local Sainsbury's; real Japanese food tastes nothing like its vacuum-wrapped Western imitations. Misawa's English isn't good enough to explain what's in front of me, which might be a good thing. Most substances are best described as squidgy and, while some are delicious, others are retch-inducing. At least Japanese beer tastes like Japanese beer.

It almost seems a shame to be slipping back into jeans next morning before we begin the assault on Mount Fuji. There are a handful of so-called '5th stations' on the volcano that can be accessed by road and form a base camp for expeditions to the top. It might sound glamorous but according to the local info it takes no more than 4hrs and 35minutes (!) to reach the top, where a gift shop awaits. In the official climbing season of July to August, as many as 3000 people a day make the ascent, so peace and solitude are not on the menu.

In the wintertime, though, all is deserted and the Fuji-Subaru line takes us up the mountain. There's a road toll of 2300 Yen (17 euros), which sounds pricey, but this proves to be one of the world's great driving roads. Quick open sections are interspersed with challenging hairpins that are a test of technique. It climbs to 2305m and the altitude puts a strain on the Nissan's 285 horses, but with the roof up, there's a greater opportunity to savour the soundtrack of the 3.5-litre V6.

We finally emerge above the cloud-line to be greeted by the snowy peak of the volcano. This is the Fuji that you see on postcards and the Nissan's temperature gauge is registering zero. Below me, the clouds roll across the horizon, blocking out the view west. By the most direct route, I am no more than 80 miles from Tokyo, but there could scarcely be a greater contrast between this desolate spot and the high-tech bustle of the capital city.

Japan is a fascinating country and the new 350Z Roadster makes a fine travelling companion. We'll reserve judgement on the dynamics until we drive a UK-spec car, but even in this guise, there seems little doubt that Nissan's engineers have succeeded in chopping off the roof without removing the car's character. This could prove to be one of the must-have cars of summer 2005.

First published on the 4Car website, 17th December 2004

RANGE ROVER SPORT TO BANGKOK

A drive from the heart of the Laos jungle to the hustle and bustle of Bangkok

Photographs WALDO VAN DER WAAL

Although Africa is my favourite continent, I've always had a soft spot for Southeast Asia. I visited Vietnam with a friend in my early twenties and met with an extraordinary country that mixed communist rule with a healthy dose of free enterprise. The scars of the Vietnam War were still evident but, on the street, the US dollar was the currency of choice. What the American military had failed to secure by force, American economic imperialism was achieving by stealth.

It would be another five years before I returned to this part of the world, but the opportunity to visit Laos was too good to miss. While the Vietnam War had captured the world's attention and provoked a thousand protest marches, the illegal, unofficial war in Laos went almost unreported. The most heavily bombed country per capita in the history of warfare suffered in silence. Even today, little is heard of this country of 6.4 million people, which is still a communist state.

My opportunity arose because of the G4 challenge, a global adventure race organised (and paid for) by Land Rover. It is a contest in which a bunch of obscenely fit athletes run, climb, kayak, drive and occasionally bungee their way across the world. I had been part of the support crew for the first G4, touring across South Africa's Garden Route and the Canyon lands of Utah, USA. Now, two years later, I was to join a recce crew as the competition sought to establish a foothold in one of the world's most beautiful and challenging countries.

Land Rover had secured a carnet to import three vehicles – two age-old Defenders and a new Range Rover Sport. The latter had only just been launched in Europe and would be driven by me. We'd start in Laos and then work our way south into Thailand and on to Bangkok, where the cars would board a cargo ship and return to the UK. In other words, I was to be part adventurer and part delivery driver.

It was a journey that would have a comedic conclusion. Bangkok is a city of considerable culture, but there can be no denying that its seedier side has earned it notoriety in the West. Pat Pong is Bangkok's most famous red light district, full of whorehouses, strip clubs and 'erotic' freak shows.

It's an extraordinary place and as we approached the city, I decided that it would make an ideal venue for a photo shoot. I hoped that a picture of the Land Rover in such a debauched environment would grab the reader's attention, while also providing a dramatic contrast with the natural, unmolested beauty of Laos.

Late at night, we arrived in Pat Pong and stopped the Sport in the middle of a congested alleyway. It was a provocative scene, but there was still something missing. Armed with 500 Thai Bhat (about £7), I approached a local ladyboy and requested that she/he pose in front of the car. The result was surely one of the most bizarre photographs ever taken, but it made the pages of Autocar.

Later that month, I filed an expense claim that read, "Ladyboy for photoshoot: 500 Bhat." One suspects this is not the first time a prostitute's fee has been hidden in an expense claim, but it is surely the first time it's been done with any degree of legitimacy.

LAND ROVER
G4
CHALLENGE
RANGE ROVER

'Van Vieng lies on the edge of the Nam Song River and is framed by dramatic limestone hilltops. Breakfast is taken watching locals potter across a small, ramshackle bridge.'

It's early evening in Van Vieng and raining with such ferocity that I fear for the safety of our Range Rover Sport. All I can do is to hide in a café and watch as the dusty roads give way to a stream of sandy mud. We simply don't get rain like this back home, global warming or not.

Van Vieng lies in Eastern Laos, some 150 miles north of the capital of Vientiane. It's a haven for backpackers, but behind the internet cafés, souvenir shops and bars lies a country living in the grip of communist rule. Even electricity is still a distant dream for most of the rural population.

Some people would say it's wrong to drive a £50,000 4x4 through here, especially one painted in such an ostentatious colour. But there is a reason for our journey. Next April, a leg of the Land Rover G4 challenge adventure race will be held in Laos, bringing with it a convoy of 60 vehicles and a welcome injection of cash.

My V8 Sport HSE is the only one in the country and was shipped out here to take part in a recce. Its work is now done and I'm tasked with driving it from Van Vieng to Bangkok, where it will board a ferry for Solihull. The journey will take us on- and off-road, from Laos's tropical jungle to the urban jungle of the Thai capital. If Land Rover's Terrain Response system was built for anything, it was for this journey.

The rain stops overnight and the sun rises to reveal one of the most beautiful natural environments in the world. Van Vieng lies on the edge of the Nam Song River and is framed by dramatic limestone hilltops. Breakfast is taken watching locals potter across a small, ramshackle bridge.

For the past few months, Land Rover's marketing gurus have been portraying the Sport as a different kind of Land Rover. This, they say, is not just another two-and-a-half tonne off-roader; this is an urbane SUV for soccer moms and cricket widows. That's why attention has focused on the 400bhp supercharged version and not on the diesel, which will account for 85 per cent of sales.

Smeared with mud and accessorised with a winch, spot lights and a roof rack, the Sport looks terrific. This car is 3000 miles from home, but it looks more comfortable in this environment than it ever will in Kensington or Chelsea. It should be the tool for the job, but I fear for the complexity of its electronic systems – if it goes wrong in the jungle, no one will hear us scream.

Most of the 'roads' in Laos are formed from orangey earth, which contrasts dramatically with the lush green landscape. We bumble along at 30-40mph with the big V8 scarcely ticking over. With the air-con maintaining a steady 20 degrees, the whole experience feels surreal: it's like I'm sitting in one of those 'experience' rides. This is a testament to the Sport's ability, but it's also an indication of how far Land Rover has travelled from its utilitarian roots.

It's also bizarre to think that 35 years ago, this country was the focal point of a secret war. From 1962 to 1973, the US, North Vietnam and China engaged in an

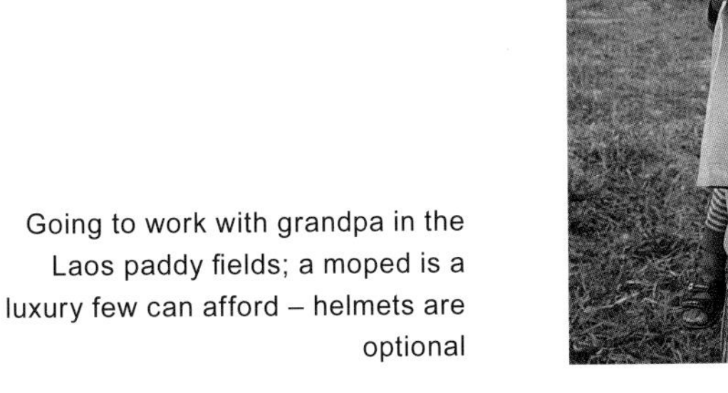

Van Vieng is a haven for western backpackers; the Sport's abilities are tested to the full on the muddy terrain

Going to work with grandpa in the Laos paddy fields; a moped is a luxury few can afford – helmets are optional

armed struggle that was in direct contravention of the Geneva Accord of 1962, which recognised the neutrality of Laos. To evade the agreement, US Air Force officers were turned into civilian pilots and Laos was referred to as the Other Theater.

Despite the secrecy, the scale of the conflict was huge: by the end of the war, the pretend air force had made Laos the most heavily bombed country, per capita, in the history of warfare. Today, the only visible reminders in this part of Laos are a handful of US military trucks and Jeeps now used by locals – a ghostly reminder of a time the West would rather forget.

We pause for fuel in the market town of Ban Tha. This is not for the faint-hearted: with little or no meaningful refrigeration available, the local traders sell most of their food live. I'm offered an iguana with its legs tied together, and a bowl of frogs with wooden spikes piercing their limbs. No less palatable was the sight of a mongoose being kept in a tiny cage as a pet.

I cross the road to inspect one of the country's most appealing curiosities. Proper vehicles are beyond the reach of most, so the locals have conjured a makeshift solution. The Tak-Tak features a simple internal combustion engine and can serve as transportation, a plough, a water pump or even as a generator. It's a one-stop shop for all your automotive needs, and it's brilliant.

The Tak-Tak has a fixed front differential, so to turn you must pull a handle to release the diff, while also operating the hand throttle and brake. I set off around some wasteland in a manner that must resemble a Monty Python sketch. A Tak-Tak is astonishingly heavy to drive and mastering one is not the work of a moment. After an aborted figure of eight, I'm happy to hand it back.

Back to Land Rover and out into the rural villages. We must reach the Thai border by 6am tomorrow. We reach the Nam Lik River, which is impassable by car. Thankfully, a small raft appears to carry us across. It's powered by a tiny outboard motor.

The enterprise is run by Bounmy, who lives on the riverbank. The ferry is open 24/7, but he receives only a handful of customers each day. When the G4 challenge is in town, he could suddenly find himself faced with transporting up to 60 vehicles. 'That would make me very happy,' he says.

Several miles later we arrive at the Nam Song River. The water is shallower here, so we raise the air suspension, select 'Rock Crawl' and wade into the river. Much to the astonishment of the locals, this luxury 4x4 simply lifts up its skirt and tiptoes across, with a minimum of fuss.

By nightfall we're in Vientiane, the closest city to Thailand, both geographically and culturally. After two days in the jungle, it feels strange to be confronted by proper streets, buildings and television, where the green shoots of capitalism are poking through.

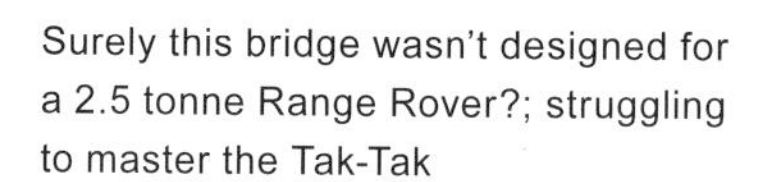

Surely this bridge wasn't designed for a 2.5 tonne Range Rover?; struggling to master the Tak-Tak

Crossing the Nam Song River, Range Rover-style

'We reach the Nam Lik River, which is impassable by car. Thankfully, a small raft appears to carry us across.'

TOUR
WIDE AIR TICKETS
,BUS, BOAT SERVICE
EL RESERVATION
VISA SERVICE
W. PAWANATOUR .COM
TATTOO
Henna Bodypainting
Nail-Hair-Extension
SUNNY FASHIONS
Ladies & Gents custom tailor
MADE TO MEASURE IN 18 HRS
WORKMANSHIP IS OUR GOAL
WELCOME TRAVEL
AUTHORIZED TRAVEL AGENT
WORLD WIDE AIR TICKETS
VISA SERVICE & SIGHT SEEING
DAILY BUS & TRAIN SERVICE
TRAVEL INSURANCE
IATA
INTERNET CAFE
OVERSEA CALL, FAX, C.D.BURNING.
K.B.
DHL
OUTLET

'Our arrival in a bright orange Land Rover is a source of amusement to the locals.'

G4
CHALLENGE
THE BIRTH PLACE OF NANAPONG
WARN
SPORT
HSE

TAXI

สก 1092
กรุงเทพมหานคร

We're up early next morning to cross the border into the Kingdom of Thailand. The Thai-Lao friendship bridge, which spans the Mekong River, was only completed in 1993 and links the two countries. It takes only a couple of minutes to cross it, but it's like entering a different age. The simple dirt roads are replaced by multi-lane highways, proper service stations and that telltale symbol of economic development, the McDonald's restaurant.

The road to Bangkok is quick, straight and undemanding, so I have time to gather my thoughts. There is no doubt the Sport has plenty of ability. It's terrific off-road, comfortable and accomplished on the highway, blessed with a stylish and comfortable cabin, and stacked with sensible equipment, especially the Terrain Response system.

Even so, I find it hard to see the point of the Range Rover Sport – beyond the snappier looks and the bling factor. A Discovery or Range Rover would have been just as effective on this trip. The Sport doesn't feel much faster and its slightly smaller body doesn't make it much more agile. All three vehicles would have tackled the off-road sections with aplomb, and the Sport's on-road dynamics aren't sufficiently different from those of the Disco to justify the hype.

Cruising along in luxury like this, you can't help regretting that contemporary Land Rovers have become largely irrelevant to the developing world. With the exception of the ancient Defender, the company's models are now too pricey and complex to be a tenable proposition in this part of the world. The Japanese have taken over. Driving through Thailand, at least, you can see an argument that the money used to build the Sport might have been better spent on a simpler and cheaper model to reconnect the brand with its roots.

I'm still pondering these things when a haze of smog on the horizon signals the arrival of Bangkok. The 'city of angels' is a heaving mass of 6 million people, most of whom are on the road. Modern vehicles, mostly Japanese saloons, mix with three-wheeler 'put-put' taxis to create an exhausting mix of heat, noise and pollution. Our arrival in a bright orange Land Rover is a source of amusement to the locals. We feel self-conscious and beat a retreat.

Next year will be different, however, when the G4 challenge proper rolls into town. The sight of 60 orange-liveried Land Rovers covered in lights and winches, all ready for one of the world's great driving challenges, will make quite a spectacle, in anyone's language. Strength in numbers.

First printed in *Autocar* magazine, 23rd August 2005

Above: Pat Pong in Bangkok – the model is not to be confused with a she

A put-put taxi ride is not to be missed; anyone for dinner?

INDIAN DRIVING TEST

Taking a driving test in Mumbai, India

Photographs STAN PAPIOR

Stories like this always carry an element of risk. What if the Indian driving test had been thorough and rigorous? What if the test car had been modern and immaculate? What if we hadn't encountered a cow or some cricketers? There was a very real danger that this story would be dull and pedestrian.

I need not have worried. This escapade was so full of slapstick humour that the story wrote itself. I had no need for hyperbole or artistic licence. The car really did have a faulty speedo and no wing mirrors; we really did encounter a bunch of cricketers; and I really was asked to perform a U-turn in a busy four-lane road. It made a good magazine story, but I reckon it would have made even better television.

This was my first visit to India and it was everything I expected. Noisy, manic, grossly overpopulated and fascinating. I arrived at around 2am to be confronted by a beggar asking for change, in any currency. The streets were populated by groups of people, wandering who knows were. And my hotel – somewhat ironically called The Ritz – seemed to have more staff than residents.

Guidebooks will tell you to drink bottled water and watch what you eat, even if you're going to Switzerland. But I've rarely taken such advice too seriously. Although I've eaten McDonald's on five continents, I reckon that tasting the local cuisine is an important part of any travelling experience. If I hadn't eaten a still-beating snake heart in Hanoi, Vietnam, then I would have offended my hosts and missed out on one of life's more bizarre moments.

In India, though, this philosophy was to be my undoing. On our last night, photographer Stan Papior and I decided to go to a comparatively swanky oriental restaurant and then on to the Hilton hotel, where we'd been invited to a social event for the ex-pat community. I ended up getting back to the Ritz at 4:30am after an impromptu party at the apartment of a Dutch diplomat.

There was nothing unusual in this. Whenever I travel, I always try to have a 'big' last night and reckon that you can learn a lot about a country by getting hammered in its bars. After this night, though, I was going to suffer.

I woke up at 9am feeling sick. After vomiting twice, I tried to recall exactly what I'd had to drink. Surely I couldn't have been that drunk? Then the diarrhoea started. It was so virulent that I almost collapsed on the bathroom floor. It felt like my whole body was trying to escape its protective skin.

My flight home was leaving in four hours and I had to be on it. Somehow I dragged myself into a taxi, clutching a bottle of water. By the time I arrived at the airport I was a shivering, sweating wreck. The flight of ten hours back to London Heathrow was the longest of my life. I sat there shaking under two blankets, unable to eat, sleep, work or even watch a movie.

It was four days before I was able to eat anything solid and I lost nearly half a stone in weight. Stories like this always carry an element of risk.

AUTOMOBILE ENGINEERS
43.M.K. ROAD BOMBAY-2.
TRESSPASSERS
Good Luck
motor t. school.
DADAR T. T. 2412 9366

Dodging Daisy on the streets of Mumbai (left); not your average road sign (above)

"You turn," says my Indian driving test examiner. "Turn where?" I ask. "No, U-turn," says the examiner, making a circular motion in the air with his finger. I glance in the rearview mirror and my interpreter, sitting on the backseat, nods his head. What can I say? I've never been to India before.

I've never driven a Maruti 800 before either, which is so small, my legs are thrust up under my chin. I must look like an oversized crab as I slide the Maruti's gearstick into 1st, ease out the clutch and begin edging my way out into the traffic. Horns blare, cars swerve and nothing seems to slow. In India, if you stop, you've had it.

We edge forward until I'm perpendicular to the traffic. A hundred green and gold taxicabs spear at me from every direction, while a huge, lumbering bus looms ever larger on the horizon. I'm scared. The Maruti has no safety belts, no airbags, and just a wafer-thin pretense of a door that separates me from bedlam.

Propelled by fear, I push on, completing the U-turn and easing my way into the torrent of traffic. A US driving test is nothing like this ...

The Good Luck Motor Training School and the Maruti

For my passenger, Hasib Khan, this is just another day at the office. For the past 15 years, he's worked as a driving examiner in Mumbai, the bustling metropolis in Southwestern India that used to be called Bombay. Khan typically tests five people each day, passing an average of three.

He works for the inspirationally named Good Luck Motor Training School, which describes itself as "a best and well-organized school with modern equipment at your service." It may well be the best school in Mumbai, but "modern equipment" is surely stretching the point.

The Maruti 800 I'm driving began life in the 1980s as a Suzuki Alto city car, but it's still one of India's best-selling cars. More than 7300 were sold in December alone, but this is not the finest example. I have no idea what the speed limit is on this section of road but neither does the car. Every time I reach about 40km/h (25mph), the speedometer gets overexcited and starts to read 130km/h (80mph). I point this out to my examiner, who grins and nods his head.

Cricket and other distractions

Khan gestures for me to turn left, which raises another concern: the car has no door mirrors. "Mr Khan says that if you had door mirrors, there would be a very high chance of damage," says my interpreter. "They have fitted a bigger centre mirror with a wide spectrum of view. That is adequate."

By peering over my shoulder, I manage a left turn and we trundle up a side street, where a game of cricket is being played. India's obsession with this strange game began under British rule and players who reach the top are feted as celebrities. Matches are played in the most bizarre places.

I'm motioned to stop in the middle of the road and Khan asks me to reverse toward a gate. Apparently, this manoeuver has only recently been added to the test and it's the reason most people fail. "The test is getting harder," says the instructor. "We are asking for more control of the car." I reverse about 5 yards before Khan nods appreciably and asks me to carry on forward.

Not enough horn

Mumbai is an exhausting place. Even if you become accustomed to the heat and the noise, it's easy to feel overwhelmed by such a concentrated mass of humanity. This is the world's most populous city; it's home to more than 14 million people and has a population density of over 29,000 per square kilometer, compared to around 10,300 in New York City.

At least half of the residents seem to be spilling out onto the road in front of me. Making progress means dodging cars, taxis, buses, motorbikes, hand carts, pedestrians and, of course, cows. Grazing happily from a rubbish skip is a giant

Don't drive on the wicket – some colonial traditions die hard

brown bovine. Hinduism is the dominant religion in Mumbai and it defines the cow as the Divine Mother of all humans. Cows are sacred and are allowed to wander freely on the streets, which is a worry. Hitting one on a driving test is not the key to eternal happiness.

I successfully negotiate my farmyard friend, but then receive my first official warning from the passenger seat. It seems that I'm making insufficient use of the horn. In India, the car's horn is a critical part of a driver's armor. Most trucks and carts carry a sign saying "horn, please" and every directional change should be accompanied by at least one audible blast of the hooter.

Swinging left at a junction, I jab frantically at the horn button on the Maruti's steering wheel, only to discover that the horn emits a pathetic "poop." If I lived in Mumbai, I'd insist on a car with a manly "parp."

A mighty 37hp

We're on a clearer stretch of road beside a railway line, and Khan encourages me to select 3rd and then 4th (top) gear. The 796cc, 37-horsepower engine sounds almost excited as we reach the dizzy heights of what must be 30mph. I glance across at my examiner, who is nodding happily but saying little. He has no notebook or crib sheet, so I have no idea how I'm doing. Can I really be failed for insufficient use of the horn?

Even at this speed, I find myself jousting with overenthusiastic taxis, which seem determined to occupy my piece of tarmac. The road quality is poor and the

vehicle's brakes are rubbish. The Maruti brochure is not wrong when it says that the 800 offers "a driving experience that's simply beyond compare."

In the best driving school tradition, the Maruti has dual controls – both the brake and clutch can be controlled from the passenger seat. Khan reckons that an accelerator would be just as useful. "I've been hit many times from behind because learners drive too slowly," he explains. "They're too cautious."

Frightening statistics

According to a local, most Indians feel safe in their cars because they rarely exceed walking pace. It's a nice theory, but it's nonsense. India's accident statistics are horrifying, with more than 85,000 killed on the roads each year, compared with around 42,500 in the US. Only China has a worse record.

It's a problem that's going to get worse. Car sales were up nearly 20 per cent in 2006 and there's plenty of scope for more growth in a country where only 1 per cent of the population has a driving license. In Mumbai, a Maruti 800 costs 205,003 rupees ($4600). At present, that's about a year's salary for a middle manager, but wages here are rising.

More cars on the road will mean extra work for the affable Mr. Khan, who is continuing his silent vigil as I crawl my way up a busy main road. The Good Luck Driving School's courses are competitively priced. Twenty lessons of 30 minute duration cost a mere 2300 rupees ($52) and my test has cost the paltry sum of 70 rupees ($1.57).

The verdict

We've now been driving for about 15 minutes and after a second death-defying U-turn, Khan directs me back in the direction of the driving school. That's it – no more tricky maneuvers, no theory questions or highway driving.

There is a lengthy exchange in Hindi before my interpreter reveals my fate. "You need to indicate more and use your horn more," he says. "But it is no problem. You drove perfectly well and very adequately for the test."

I've passed and can now look forward to a lifetime of driving in India. Which is great news ... I think.

'Mumbai is an exhausting place. Even if you become accustomed to the heat and the noise, it's easy to feel overwhelmed by such a concentrated mass of humanity ... At least half of the residents seem to be spilling out onto the road in front of me.'

DADAR T.T. 2412 9366

JAGUAR XK TO SYDNEY

A 2000 mile drive across the southwest corner of Australia

Photographs ALISTAIR WEAVER

After every foreign adventure, there's a question I always ask myself: "Would I want to live there?" It's a fun game to play and it sometimes throws up some surprising answers.

I've decided, for example, that I would like to live in Hanoi (Vietnam) but not in Bangkok, (Thailand). Hong Kong would appeal more than Tokyo, and I definitely wouldn't want to reside in Beijing. A mud hut village in Zambia would offer a different perspective on life, but I couldn't live behind a barbed-wire fence in South Africa.

If I decide that I might want to live somewhere, I ask myself a supplementary question: "For how long?" Places then tend to fall into two categories – those where I would like to live for a couple of years, and those where I could conceivably settle down.

For an Anglophile like me, most places fall into the first category. Rio de Janeiro, for example, would be fascinating for a while, but I can't see myself growing old there. Likewise Le Paz and Milan.

Only a handful of places fall into the second category. I've often toyed with the idea of moving to the US. New York is my favourite city and I'd love to live there. I could also see myself settling down in Los Angeles. LA has the advantage of the Californian climate, while New York is cool and cosmopolitan.

The other country where I'd always suspected I'd enjoy living is Australia. There are lots of Aussies where I live in London, and I've always admired their determination, humour and passion for sport; but it wasn't until New Year 2007 that I finally travelled 'Down Under'.

There were two factors drawing me to Australia at this time: my girlfriend – who'd taken four months out to travel – and cricket. Two years earlier, the English cricket team had beaten the mighty Australia to regain the famous Ashes. Now, they had to defend them on the Aussies' home turf. Large swathes of the world have never really understood the appeal of leather on willow, but for Aussies and Poms, this was one of the most eagerly anticipated sporting occasions of all time.

The cricket turned out to be an abject disaster – England lost the Test Series 5-0 and became the butt of a thousand jokes – but I fell for the country. I spent New Year in Sydney before heading to Adelaide to start my drive. And when it was over, I spent a few happy days on a boat in the Whitsunday Islands, on the edge of the Great Barrier Reef. The latter is not to be missed, especially if you enjoy diving.

What made this trip even more fun was that it was so accessible. The drive from Adelaide to Sydney was the easiest of all my adventures to achieve, but that didn't make it any less fun.

NSW
AYF·77M

Adelaide is little more than a town. But despite having a population of fewer than 1,500,000 people, by night it throbs to the beat of 100 bars and restaurants. And from the centre of town, it's just a few miles to Australia's southern coastline, where surf bums practise their art.

For a penal colony, it has huge appeal.

It's also the starting point for the long journey from Adelaide to Sydney. Stick to the highway and this is a drive of around 1000 miles. However, to do so would be to miss some of the world's most spectacular scenery. And given the Australian predilection for speed limits, it would also be a monumentally boring and frustrating drive, especially when your car for the journey is a Jaguar XK.

The Jag, like me, is 8000 miles from home, but it looks more at ease here than I ever could. While I lack tan, tone and attitude, the Jag looks svelte, cool and appealing. It even looks contemporary – and when was the last time you thought that of a Jaguar?

After leaving Adelaide, we get our first taste of the extraordinary scale of this country. This is high season in one of the most densely populated areas of the country, but we can still drive for miles without seeing another person as we flash by the gentle, rolling countryside in search of the tiny port of Robe. It's a somewhat undistinguished town, famous for one thing – lobster. Caught fresh on a daily basis, the crustaceans here are said to be the best in the world and, after a hearty dinner, washed down with local Chardonnay, it's difficult to disagree.

We ditch the coastline next morning and plot a route to the Grampians National Park, which separates the coastal region from the Australian Outback. The drive reminds me of the US. Quiet, wide open highways link nondescript low-rise towns that, if you were feeling uncharitable, you would call hick.

Our home for the night is an Aquila Eco Lodge. Part of Australia's burgeoning eco-tourism industry, it's owned and run by the genial Barb Bjerking. The Lodges are powered by biodiesel produced from the cooking oil used by local restaurants. Water is collected from the rooftops and the waste is processed by worms. 'The only line into Aquila is the telephone line,' she says with pride.

Cruising back from an evening meal, we have our first contact with one of Australia's most famous inhabitants. There are signs dotted along the roads warning of kangaroos, but nothing quite prepares you for the sight of them in the wild. They are such unlikely, comic creatures. The first time you see one 'boing' for real, I challenge you not to laugh.

From the Grampians, we return to the coast and join the Great Ocean Road, which links the towns of Warrnambool and Torquay. The road attracts seven million tourists each year and most of them seem to be here today. The Jaguar was made for a trip like this. It follows the classic GT recipe, with a large-capacity V8, a 2+2 cabin and a sensible boot. There's so much to enjoy about this car. The 300bhp engine sounds terrific and it drives well. It's not as overtly sporting as a Porsche 911, but it's more engaging than a Mercedes SL and more comfortable than a BMW 6-Series. It is, in other words, well judged.

The focal point of the Great Ocean Road is the series of lonely, dramatic rock stacks known as the Twelve Apostles, the result of an eroding coastline. Today, the name seems something of a misnomer, because only six of the Apostles are visible from the viewing platform. They are a magnificent sight ruined only by the plague of flies that engulf the coastline; they're so annoying that I'm tempted to buy a Crocodile Dundee hat, complete with corks.

Back to the Jaguar and on towards Torquay, the seaside town that has nothing in common with its British namesake made famous by the hapless Basil Fawlty – certainly not the temperature, which today is an outrageously hot 44 degrees according to the XK's thermometer. This is a coastline prone to shark attacks. Just three weeks ago, a boy lost a leg when he was bitten close to Torquay. All of this is a concern, given that I've just booked a surf lesson. If the heat doesn't get me, Jaws might.

‘The Jag, like me, is 8000 miles from home, but it looks more at ease here than I ever could.’

According to my impossibly healthy-looking instructor, Luke Slater, the surf conditions are 'not ideal for beginners' and, at 6'4", I'm 'a bit too tall'. To no-one's surprise, I take to surfing like a duck to an arid desert. I'd like to tell you what its like to stand up and ride the waves, but I can't, because I can't. But it is good fun.

From Torquay, we pick up the main highway to Melbourne, which proves to be a surreal experience due to the Australian authorities' zeal for speed enforcement. Even if you're only 4kmh over the limit, you will most likely be nicked. Instead of powering past large trucks, cars creep past, exposing their passengers to greater danger.

Australia also has a huge problem with drivers falling asleep at the wheel: 100km/h (62mph) on a clear three-lane highway feels ridiculously slow. Drivers simply apply their cruise control and switch off. I see one chap driving with his feet on the dashboard. The policy might make more sense if it was consistent. In South Australia, the speed limit is 110km/h, but in Victoria it's 100km/h. So is 104km/h lethal or isn't it?

Melbourne is a terrific city. More than twice the size of Adelaide, it's also much more cosmopolitan. There is an arty, almost hedonistic feel to some of the neighbourhoods, especially those by the beach.

And it's home to the hit soap opera, Neighbours, with tours of the real-life street set run daily. My tour is filled with thirtysomething Brits, all glorying in the naffness of it. 'Ramsay Street' is actually called Pin Oak Court and it's a honey trap for tourists. The residents, who receive an income from the show, had to hire a full-time security guard after two British backpackers were caught having rumpy in Harold Bishop's front garden.

Every time I return to the XK, I follow the same routine. I admire the styling, grin at the raspy exhaust note and frown at the interior. It's comfortable and spacious (for two people) but it just doesn't feel special enough for a car that costs £59,000. Too many of the plastics feel like they were chosen for their cost, not their quality. There is no sense of occasion.

The radio aerial is also an aberration. Every time you switch on the stereo, an aerial emerges from the right rear wing, just like it used to when Elvis was a lad. Jaguar argues that it's needed to ensure proper reception in the US, but when was the last time you saw one on a Merc or Bee Em? I cringe whenever I catch sight of it in the rear-view mirror. Jaguar is apparently working on a solution.

From Melbourne, we take another journey inland to the old gold mining town of Walhalla. The road that climbs up the mountain offers a terrific challenge. The XK is undoubtedly at its best on wide sweeping highways, but it's happy to roll up its sleeves when needs must. And I suspect that it would feel even better on this road if our car had been fitted with the optional electronic damping.

Not far from our destination, I'm surprised to be met by trucks full of blackened faces travelling in the opposite direction.

'The bush fire is only 5km away,' says Michael Leaney, the owner of the Walhalla Star Hotel. They're 'back burning' – deliberately clearing areas of woodland to try to protect the town.

Leaney shows us a map of the area, which displays the extent of the fire. More than 900,000 hectares of bush have been lost, an area equivalent to a quarter of Switzerland. Part of the town's historic railway has already been destroyed and it will cost $250,000 to replace. To make matters worse, the tourists are staying away. It is sobering stuff.

We leave Walhalla mid-morning and return to the coast road, stopping at the Paperbark Camp. Guests stay in huge safari tents, imported from Africa and dine with possums in a restaurant on stilts. Populated by tourists and stressed-out Sydney types, this is 'posh camping' at its very best.

From the Paperbark, we take the coast road once more towards Sydney. This is my final day with the Jag, a car that really captures the imagination. Every day

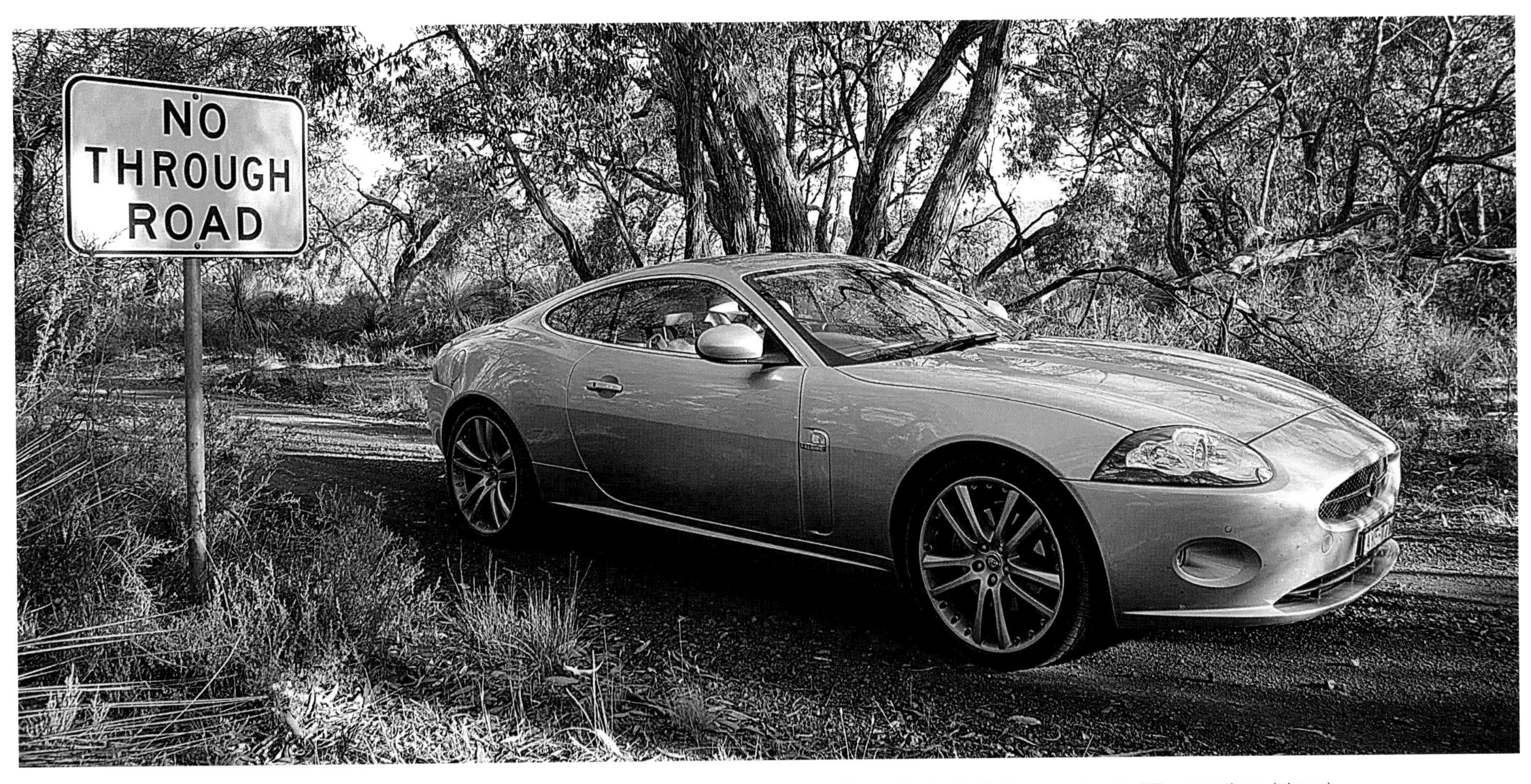

Kangaroos are both a national treasure and a hazard; buskers start young Down Under (left); Jag has classic GT proportions (above)

NSW
AYF·77M

'This is my final day with the Jag, a car that really captures the imagination. Every day I'm engaged in conversation about the car and the reaction has been almost wholly positive. This is the best car that Jaguar has made in at least a generation.'

I'm engaged in conversation about the car and the reaction has been almost wholly positive. This is the best car that Jaguar has made in at least a generation. Only the cabin trim and that stupid aerial let it down.

Finally, after more than a week on the road, the city of Sydney fills the view beyond the bonnet. We make for McMahon's Point, which offers a unique view across Sydney Harbour to the iconic bridge and opera house. It is a fitting place in which to end what has been a fascinating journey.

The drive we have just completed is easy to accomplish. Anyone flying to Sydney or Adelaide could rent a car and make a similar trip. But just because it's easy doesn't make it less interesting. This part of Australia is a land of immense natural beauty and surprising contrasts. If you have a couple of weeks to spare and can stomach the 20-hour flight, do it.

First published on the 4Car website, 19th March 2007

BMW X3 IN SOWETO

Two days in the South African township of Soweto

Photographs WALDO VAN DER WAAL

In April 2003, I found myself in Johannesburg airport with a few hours to kill before my return to the UK. My travelling companion was the PR Director of Land Rover, Andrew Roberts, and together we hatched a plan to tour the city. We hired a cab and asked the driver to show us the city's focal points, both good and bad.

After a tour of central Johannesburg – a city full of hatred and despair – we travelled to Soweto, the township that had been built to house black labour. In days gone by, its population had been transient – people stayed as long as they had work – but that had changed since the end of apartheid. Many people now owned their own homes and the rows of neat little houses all seemed to have their own story to tell. This town of Nelson Mandela and Archbishop Desmond Tutu was living history and I vowed to return.

The opportunity arose a couple of years later when I passed through Johannesburg on my way back from a visit to Zambia. My photographer friend, Waldo van der Waal, had returned to his native South Africa from the UK and said he would be happy to accompany me. He even persuaded BMW to lend us a car.

Waldo is a powerfully-built white South African and had last visited Soweto a decade earlier, when he'd been working as a war reporter. "Nobody pulls a gun in Johannesburg unless they mean to use it," he explained. In common with most of his contemporaries, Waldo owns a hand gun, but we didn't take it to Soweto. Instead, he gave me a CFC pepper spray that I was to use if attacked.

The trip proved to be just as fascinating as I'd hoped. Although it retained a definite edge, there was also a spirit of optimism. Almost everyone we met was happy to talk to us and we were never threatened. Indeed, I had forgotten that Waldo had given me the pepper spray until I arrived at airport security.

Trying to explain to an airport official in the post-9/11 world that I really wasn't trying to board a 'plane with a potentially disabling weapon was quite a challenge. I suspect British or American security staff would have been less understanding.

The Soweto story ran first in Autocar *magazine in the UK, and I was surprised to receive some criticism. Some of my contemporaries felt the story was in bad taste and that I'd come dangerously close to poking fun at poverty. It made me question whether I'd done the right thing and, equally, whether I should include the story in this book.*

In the end, I applied the same test that I have always applied when addressing such issues: would the people involved have opposed the story? In this instance, I can answer with considerable confidence that they would not.

PLAY GEAR
S
STREET
SPORT

Small, brightly coloured houses are a feature of Sowetan life (right); our X3 suffers altitude sickness (above)

My South African friends are betting on how long we'll survive in Soweto and the big money is on four hours. Carjacking in the township is rife and two white men in a brand new BMW X3 are an obvious and vulnerable target. But even if they take the car, I'll be okay, yeah? 'Not necessarily,' says a friend. 'Sometimes they just shoot the driver and then drag out the body.'

This is starting to sound like a bad idea. Back in the comfort and relative security of London, I'd come up with the idea of using BMW's latest 4x4 to explore the famous township that this year celebrates its 100th anniversary. But what promised to be a fascinating journey into the world of the Mandelas and Archbishop Desmond Tutu now feels like an act of stupidity.

And my nerves are well and truly jangling when photographer Waldo hands me a canister filled with pepper spray. 'If you're attacked, just spray it in their face,' he says helpfully. Waldo lives in Johannesburg, but it's been 10 years since he last visited Soweto. Back then, he was working as a war correspondent, and he wore a flak jacket permanently. This will, he promises, be a very 'real' experience.

We meet our guide, Thamsanqa Nndimande, at a McDonald's just outside Soweto. Thami will accompany us throughout the trip and, in theory, deal with any problems that may arise. He hops into the X3's passenger seat and starts directing me through a complex maze of streets that spans over 46 square miles and is home to around 3.5 million black South Africans.

The name Soweto is actually an acronym for South Western Township. Twenty miles from the centre of Johannesburg it was built as a 'dormitory' for black workers who stayed as long as they had a job. It wasn't until 1994 and the end of apartheid that the locals were given freehold rights to their properties.

'Deep Soweto used to be like the Wild West,' says Thami, 'but now that people own their own houses, they've started to take a pride in the town.' It's Sunday evening and the BMW's xenon bulbs cast a weird blue light on the massed rows of small, rectangular houses. Built in brick, they're roughly the size of a double garage – yet they house Soweto's middle class.

We've been driving for 20 minutes when we arrive at the famous Vilakazi street. Archbishop Desmond Tutu still owns a house on one corner and Nelson Mandela lived here before he was jailed in '63. No other street in the world can claim two Nobel Peace Prize winners.

Time for a quick meal before heading out in to the Sowetan night. Much to my relief, Thami is delighted with our choice of vehicle. 'There is an illegal street race here every Thursday night,' he explains. 'There's a big car culture in Soweto and BMW is the favourite make. Everyone wants a (1980s) 325is – we call it the matchbox car.' Some of these cars, our guide accepts, may have arrived in Soweto by less than honest means. 'We call it the repossession of assets,' he says. Later in the evening, we spot a 'matchbox', parked outside a trendy bar.

I'm starting to feel more confident – but this veneer is shattered at 4am when I'm awakened by gunfire. It is loud. Close. I try to convince myself that I'm just a paranoid tourist, that it couldn't have been a machine gun, but Thami confirms my suspicions.

Early morning in Soweto (right) – most buses head for nearby Johannesburg

'There are local gangs,' he says. 'It's not unusual for them to shoot at one another.'

It's a relief to find the X3 where I left it, with no new holes. Life in Soweto kicks into gear at around 6am, when many begin their two-hour commute to work in Johannesburg. The central bus station doubles as a marketplace and is located opposite the gigantic Chris Hani Baragwanath hospital, which cares for 3000 ward patients and is the largest in the southern hemisphere. We arrive at a little after 6am to find the area already swamped with a throbbing, buzzing mass of humanity.

Tired minibuses battle for space and attention as street vendors clamour for customers. In such company, the X3 looks horribly conspicuous. I'm the only white person for miles around and I'm sitting in an ostentatious vehicle that costs around £35,000. The guide book would call it madness, but the reaction to my presence is favourable. One fearsome-looking chap even pauses to offer me a thumbs up.

Abandoning the car, I take a stroll through the marketplace. You can buy everything from razors to peanuts here, but my eye is taken by a steaming pile of what appear to be animal parts.

'They're called smilies,' explains the stall-holder. 'They're sheep's heads and you mix them with salt and bread.' Half a smiley costs just seven rand (about 60p) – a bargain, but for some reason I'm not so hungry now.

The local *Daily Sun* newspaper is also on sale at this stall. Taking its lead from its British namesake, the front page is shared between the do! Bang! Bang! story about a groom who shot his bride on their wedding day, and a piece about mini-skirts. According to the paper, 'mini-skirts and flashy G-strings are so disturbing to taxi drivers that women who show off what they've got have been warned not to sit where the driver can see them.' I can't imagine the average British cabbie objecting to short skirts.

Returning to the X3, we head across town in search of one of Soweto's wealthier districts. Driving here is surprisingly easy. The roads are in good condition, there's little traffic and the few cars tend to move in an orderly manner. But while the conditions are good, the altitude has a major effect on the engine. In the UK, the X3's 2.5-litre motor musters 192bhp but here, at 5750ft, it's more like 157bhp and the car feels slothful.

But it does have a very cool nickname. We stop at a hand carwash where Thami tells me that contemporary BMWs, such as the X3, are known as G-string cars in Soweto. This has nothing to do with their power to attract the opposite sex and everything to do with the shape of the grille. Have a look and you'll notice that the slither of metal between the vents forms a shape that resembles a string.

The Sowetans have a nickname for just about every desirable car. The hugely popular VW Golf VR6 is called a 'virus'; a BMW M Coupé looks like a designer shoe and is therefore a 'Byblos boot'. But my favourite is the locals' name for a taxi. These invariably tatty cars are called 'Zola Budds' because they're South African and run fast.

We spot a couple of 'viruses' here, an area which boasts a sprinkling of houses that look like they've been lifted from Beverley Hills. Winnie Mandela's heavily protected mansion is the township's biggest dwelling. The so-called Castle of Soweto

BJZ246 GP
MHX414 GP
RJS 692 GP

Car culture is alive and well in Soweto, even among the young; Be'Ems are ripe for 'repossession'

is worth more than £250,000 – a huge sum in South Africa. Thami explains that these homes are owned by the 'Cheddars' or 'Cheese boys' – so-called because they fill their fridges with cheese when everyone else makes do with bread and water. 'Everyone wants to be a Cheddar.'

Little more than 500 yards from the Castle is the dormitory accommodation that houses Soweto's migrant labour force. These people go without electricity and fetch their water from a communal tap. Many families are also forced to live in makeshift slums made of corrugated iron. Unemployment in Soweto is estimated to be around 40 per cent and there's no system of social security. Many of those born between 1976 and 1994 – the so-called Generation X – suffer bleak prospects indeed. It's little wonder that crime is commonplace or that life is cheap.

It's impossible to escape Soweto's poverty, just as it is impossible to escape the haunting spectre of Aids. Estimates suggest that 35 per cent of Sowetans are HIV positive and there are billboards everywhere encouraging the use of condoms. 'Everyone knows someone who's died, or is dying, of Aids,' says Thami, 'but this is still a promiscuous society.'

Still, most of the Sowetans we meet tell us that they're optimistic about the future. And much of this is to do with the changing political landscape. 'Officially, young blacks like me are called PDIs or Previously Disadvantaged Individuals,' he says, 'but I prefer to call myself a CEO for 'Currently Exposed to Opportunities – it sounds more positive.'

I had arrived in Soweto concerned about my ostentatious transport, but the X3 had turned out to be a great facilitator. Instead of provoking suspicion, it provoked interest. Young men in particular have been fascinated by this new G-string and anxious to talk cars. Soweto might be famous for its feelings of resentment, but there is also plenty of aspiration. The X3 is not my favourite BMW, but today I've been grateful for its presence.

It's getting dark again and we drop Thami at home and begin the long drive out of Soweto. Without our guide, I start to feel uneasy again. On the approach to every red traffic light I hang back, hoping we won't have to stop. Maybe I'm being paranoid, but the sound of gunfire still rings in my ears.

Soweto is clearly not the battleground it once was. There is now a discernable upper-middle class which can realistically aspire to own cars like the X3. But while some have done well, it's equally clear that for the very poor, life has changed little since the time of apartheid. Waldo was right – this was very 'real'.

First printed in *Autocar* magazine, 11th January 2005

FNB
RJS 692 GP

BENTLEY TO THE DIAMOND MINES

How a hole in the South African landscape saved Bentley

Photographs WALDO VAN DER WAAL

It often makes me laugh when people talk about a car's 'nationality'- "That car is as British as roast beef and Yorkshire puddings," etc. etc. When Aston Martin was recently sold by Ford, it was hailed in some quarters as being returned to 'British hands'. But while the Chairman, David Richards, is British, the CEO is German, and most of the money came from Kuwait. In today's world, capital has become such a global commodity that there is almost no such thing as a 'home grown' marque.

Aston's main rival in the sports luxury sector is Bentley, and much has been made in recent years of its German ownership. Volkswagen bought Bentley from Vickers back in 1998 as part of the deal that four years later saw BMW take ownership of Rolls Royce. The company founded by W O Bentley continues to make cars in Crewe, England, but its CEO (Dr Franz-Josef Paefgen) is a German, and the key decisions about its future are made in Wolfsburg, the birthplace of Hitler's Beetle.

The deal was critical for securing Bentley's future as a brand. Bentley has benefited enormously from clever stewardship and a growth in the global demand for luxury goods. Even the puritans who bemoan the new Continental's VW underpinnings are forced to admit that Bentley's future is now more secure than at almost any other point in its topsy-turvy history. Better a German Bentley than no Bentley at all.

For me, the irony of the whole 'ownership' debate was thrown into sharper focus by the revelation that, had it not been for a hole in the South African landscape, Bentley would almost certainly not have survived the 1920s. Woolf Barnato is best remembered as the Bentley Boy who won Le Mans on three successive occasions (1928-30), but it was his financial input that kept the company solvent. And this fortune was secured in the South African diamond mines of the 1880s.

It was a fascinating revelation that seemed worthy of a trip to South Africa, one of my favourite countries. Bentley kindly agreed to lend me a car, which I was to collect from a dealership in Johannesburg. This made me slightly uneasy. Carjacking is rife in Johannesburg and a white foreigner in a new Bentley would surely be a potent target.

"Don't worry," said Waldo, my photographer friend and a Johannesburg resident. "A Bentley is too otherworldly. It is too conspicuous; they could never sell it on." Apparently, Waldo's Audi A3 was more of a target than a Bentley Continental GT.

Spearing across dirt roads at 100mph plus in the first of the 'German' Bentleys was a stark reminder of the pace of progress in the automotive industry. As a British officer in the Royal Field Artillery during the First World War, one suspects that Woolf would have been less than enthralled by the nationality of Bentley's latest owner, but he would also surely have had respect for the kind of car the company's now producing.

On 14 June 1897, Barney Barnato was drowned at sea en route to England. The record books show that the cockney, who made a fortune in the South African diamond mines, committed suicide, but legend says he was pushed. Murdered or not, Barney's death was to have a dramatic impact not just on South Africa, but on the future of one of Britain's most prestigious car companies … Bentley.

Accompanying Barney on the ocean liner was his 2 year-old son, Woolf, who inherited his father's millions. Thirty-one years later, Woolf would win Le Mans for Bentley, a feat he repeated in 1929 and 1930. The son and heir was the archetypal playboy Bentley Boy, but he was also Chairman of the company. In 1926, his investment had rescued Bentley, and he would continue to pour huge sums into his pet project until it was sold to Rolls-Royce in 1931.

Today, Barnato's open cast mine, known as the "big hole", can still be seen in the town of Kimberley, South Africa. Were it not for this ugly crevasse, Bentley might not exist, which is why I've travelled 3000 miles to pay my respects. For the next two days, we'll be touring the area in a modern Continental GT, the car that Barney might have been driving, had he been around today.

The 350 mile drive from Johannesburg to Kimberely has been hugely instructive. South Africa's biggest city is now an ugly hotbed of racial and economic tension. The ghost of apartheid, coupled with a huge disparity between rich and poor, has created a culture of violence. Car-jacking is rife but, perversely, a Continental GT is too expensive and too conspicuous to be a target … or so I'm told.

To leave the city limits, though, is to discover a different South Africa. The barren, dusty landscape can have changed little since Barney arrived here in 1873, armed with £50 and a box of cheap cigars. He joined his brother Harry in a comedy duo, performing Shakespeare in a cockney accent, before diamonds caught their eye. But where Barney travelled on dirt tracks by horse and cart, we journey by W12 on a Tarmac highway.

The roads – straight, fast and sparsely populated – could have been designed for the Continental GT. Too often in Europe a grand tour means cruising from one traffic jam to the next, but in South Africa you really can average big speeds. We cruised at 100mph on the run from Johannesburg, conscious that we were using only half the Bentley's potential. The Conti really is a proper GT – it's difficult to think of another coupé that's such a capable, comfortable tool. A journey that would have taken Barney at least a week, took us five hours.

Diamonds were first discovered in Kimberley in 1866 and, by the 1880s,

From dust to dusk – century-old mine dumps are reprocessed; Continental GT is the first of the 'German' Bentleys

the place was buzzing. This was only the fourth town in the world to benefit from electric street lighting, but, like America's Wild West, it also had a reputation for vice. Bars outnumbered churches two-to-one and the town's most famous prostitute, Diamond Lil, chose her clients by the size of their rocks.

Lil has long since passed away and, today, the town is a sprawling mess of ugly buildings. Few tourists visit, although the De Beers diamond company is investing 50 million rand (c.£4.5 million) in a bid to change that. Maybe these new-found visitors will also be attracted to what is claimed to be one of only four drive-in bars in the world. Cecil Rhodes once turned up on horseback demanding a pint, but today's visitors hoot their horns for service. It's tempting to try it in the Bentley, but we're too self-conscious.

Having given up on Shakespeare, the Barnatos became "Kopje wallopers" – purchasing and processing diamonds others had neglected. The ploy quickly made them rich and they began buying up claims in the Kimberley Diamond Mine. By 1880, the Barnato Brothers Diamond Mining Company had become the Kimberley Central Diamond Mining Company, and was now finding £9000 worth of diamonds each month.

Up the road from the Kimberley Mine was the De Beers Mine, named after the farmers who originally owned the land. This was run by Cecil Rhodes, who was busy building a fortune before going on to become the only man in history to have two countries and a confederation named after him. The battle for hegemony between Rhodes, the middleclass, Oxford-educated son of a vicar, and Barnato, the hard drinking cockney Jew was to become the Kimberley soap opera of the 1880s.

In a man's world, Barney was more man than most, and the contrast between his and Woolf's early life could not be greater. Woolf had several homes, including one in London's Berkeley Square; he bred horses, threw legendary parties and won Le Mans. Barney liked a fight so much that he had his own boxing academy and was blackballed when he tried to join the upmarket Kimberley Club.

It's difficult to imagine what father or son would have thought of the Continental GT. Much ink has been used describing its VW Phaeton-derived underpinnings and debating whether or not it's a proper Bentley. For what it's worth, I couldn't care less whether its air suspension was sourced from Germany or Timbuktu. What matters is whether the sum of its parts add up to a great car that does justice to the Bentley nameplate.

After a day behind the wheel, I'm still to be convinced. On one level,

'The telltale silhouette of a conveyer belt on the horizon suggests we've found what we're looking for. Driving closer, we discover a scene reminiscent of a Mad Max movie.'

Rudi Raath used to be an electrical engineer before he became a diamond hunter (top left); three wise ladies, and a Bentley (right)

the interior is a revelation: it's packed with modern gizmos, the rear seats are genuinely useful, and it feels like it will last a millennium. But it is also utterly devoid of character. It's almost as if the designers have crammed in as many traditional Bentley design cues as possible in the hope that they will create an authentic feel.

Sadly, the overall impression is of an interior that tries too hard. The chrome air vents jar with the ultra modern infotainment interface, while the aluminium door releases are so curvaceous that they could only have been crafted by a machine. And the leather is so perfect that you suspect it will never fade or crack, like old leather should. While Aston Martin has produced a contemporary interior with an appropriate feel, Bentley has delivered a pastiche.

Next morning, we travel to the edge of town to a small open-air museum beside Barney's "Big Hole." It's here that the boxing academy has been faithfully reproduced and where De Beers is focusing its investment. Building work is already under way to create an interactive tribute to the diamond pioneers – think Beamish with a sparkle. Inside, we're greeted by Mervyn Ward, Secretary of the De Beers Consolidated Mines Company.

The De Beers that Ward represents can still be traced back to a company created by Rhodes in 1889, the year in which he finally outfoxed his old rival to secure the Kimberley diamond mine and take control of the region. Rhodes wrote a cheque for an astonishing £5,338,650 to secure the foundation of De Beers Consolidated Mines Ltd, which became the largest company the world had ever seen. Barney might have lost his war with Rhodes, but he was now one of the world's richest men, and a Life Governor of the new De Beers.

"Since those days, Kimberley has been the registered office of De Beers and it's where the board meetings are held," says Ward. "This place is dear to our hearts. We still employ 2500-3000 people here and we still mine. Last year, we produced over 2 million carats from the Kimberley mine, which is the highest figure since 1914." The Secretary invites us to view the company boardroom, where Rhodes' cheque is proudly displayed. It's an amazing curiosity.

Leaving the oak-walled splendour of De Beers, we travel in search of a group of independent miners, who keep alive the spirit of those original pioneers. Getting there means ditching the Tarmac highway for some of the dirt roads that criss-cross rural South Africa. On this loose surface, the Bentley feels incredibly composed, with its air suspension and four-wheel drive systems blending to fine effect. No 200mph car with 552bhp and 479lb ft of torque has any right to feel this sure-

footed, this safe. I find myself sprinting across compacted earth at 110mph in a car that costs 2.55 million rand (£232k) in South Africa.

The telltale silhouette of a conveyer belt on the horizon suggests we've found what we're looking for. Driving closer, we discover a scene reminiscent of a *Mad Max* movie. There's a battered old caravan, a collection of age-old construction equipment, and several piles of dirt. These diamond seekers don't dig in a conventional sense. Instead, they buy a permit from De Beers to reprocess century-old mine dumps.

"The systems they used back then were very primitive, so they tended to miss a lot," says Rudi Raath. "We have a team of ten people and we earn a decent living." Raath used to be an electrical engineer, but "got sick of the corporate life." The 41 year-old now hunts for diamonds with his wife, his brother (an ex-HR specialist) and their 72 year-old father.

"You find a 6 or 7 carat diamond now and again," he says. "Some people get lucky and find a 30 or 40 carat diamond. If it comes around, it comes around." Using a simple but effective sieving technique, the brothers pick out even the smallest diamond. It's fascinating to watch these highly educated men sifting through piles of dirt in search of buried treasure.

We motion to leave, only to be stopped by one of Raath's friends and rivals, Gavin Ricketts. "Why," he asks, "did you bring a beautiful car like that into a dirty shit place like this?" It's a fair question.

Pointing the Continental in the direction of Johannesburg, we make a bid for home. We've another 400 miles to go, on a mix of dirt road and Tarmac, but it's no hardship. This Bentley is a fantastic long distance machine, but for all its technical brilliance, it still leaves me cold. The engine is so quiet and the steering so lifeless that you feel detached from the experience.

I've never subscribed to the theory that a car must have flaws to have 'character', but a car this expensive should offer something beyond mere competency. Whereas the DB9 provokes feelings of wanton lust, the Continental GT seems clinical and contrived. Woolf Barnato, who died young in 1948, would not have recognised the Bentley of today, any more than his father would have understood contemporary South Africa. But one suspects the Barnatos would have been proud of their role in the history of both. Next time someone moans about Bentley's German parentage, just remind them that were it not for a hole in the South African landscape and the tragic death of a cockney, the company wouldn't even exist.

First printed in *Octane* magazine, September 2007

LAND ROVER ACROSS TANZANIA & KENYA

Chasing poachers from the Masai Steppe to the slopes of Mount Kenya

Photographs TOM SALT

There is a story behind the story of my visit to Tanzania. Our original intention had been to use a bespoke Land Rover developed for the survival specialist and TV celebrity Ray Mears. This Defender had been equipped with a tent on the roof and all manner of domestic accoutrements.

The first indication that things might not go according to plan had come a few days before we left. We were told the car was stuck in Tanzanian customs and there was a chance it might not be released before we arrived. Nevertheless, we should travel. Photographer Tom and I flew to Nairobi in Kenya, from where I called my contact in Dar es Salaam. He said the vehicle was still on the dock but that he was working on it. I should come to Tanzania to sort it out.

We flew to Dar es Salaam and met the contact in our hotel bar. There was, he told me, no chance of the vehicle being released and that he had known this for several days. Never in all my travels have I come closer to punching someone. I found myself pacing round the hotel, trying to contain my fury while Tom tried to make sense of it all.

It was a hopeless situation – even our attempts at bribery failed. We were in Africa, we had no vehicle and our only return ticket was from Nairobi. After frantic negotiation, we managed to borrow a Land Rover Defender from the Born Free Foundation. We would be accompanied by the fabulous Winnie Kiiru from the Foundation, who would introduce us to the Masai, Joseph Lendiy.

Out of adversity came a fascinating trip. Lendiy is an extraordinary man who'd been born in a Masai village, studied in the US, worked for the Tanzanian government and then returned to his village. His views on Africa were fascinating. Instead of blaming imperialism, capitalism or corruption for the continent's plight, he felt the Africans had to accept most of the responsibility. If his views had been expressed by a politician in the developed world, they'd have been called racist.

Both Lendiy and Kiiru – an affluent black Kenyan – were also concerned about the Western media's portrayal of Africa. The focus, they felt, is always on poverty and deprivation. "We're really a very happy people – we don't have much, but we share what we do have," reckoned Kirru.

It is a view with which I have considerable sympathy. There is an undeniable spirit about the African people that puts to shame the affluent West, and that's why it's my favourite continent. Too many people are willing to portray Africans as sad and repressed in order to meet their own political ends.

A few weeks later, Land Rover decided to have the 'Ray Mears' Defender shipped back to the UK. Neither Mears nor myself had managed to extricate it from the vice-like grip of the Tanzanian customs. It was an important lesson that when you're travelling, especially in the Third World, nothing can be taken for granted.

KAQ 156B

Age-old Defender is the perfect tool for this environment; this elephant has been slaughtered for its ivory tusks

One story about Kilimanjaro has it that Queen Victoria gave it to Kaiser Wilhelm after he complained that she had two mountains and he none. As ruler of Kenya, she made a quick squiggle on the map to include it as part of its neighbour, Tanzania, a German dominion. Charming gift though it was for her cousin, it must have been spoiled somewhat by an inability to find a display case up to the job.

The story's not true, of course. It probably comes from the pen of a contemporary satirist, keen to point out the vainglorious absurdities at the heart of the scramble for Africa. Sitting chewing on some cooked goat in Tinga Tinga, about 10 miles from the great mountain, the reverberations of such expansionism can still be felt, though on a more positive note, at least it's two-way traffic these days. There's my Masai guide, Joseph Lendiy, born in a local village but educated at the Colorado State University in the USA. He later returned to Tanzania, where he now runs the East Kilimanjaro Fieldman project, an organisation that seeks to protect the traditions and culture of the Masai. And there's the Land Rover Defender parked a few metres away from us, looking as relevant and purposeful out here in the bush as it does affected in Chelsea.

I was in Tanzania to catch up with the Born Free Foundation, a charitable organisation that works to preserve the African wildlife, and a name most people will know from the 1964 film. The BFF, as well the Tanzanian authorities, uses the expertise of people like Joseph Lendiy to help it prevent the illegal poaching that continues to threaten the survival of some of the region's most precious species. Our plan is to take the Defender from Kilimanjaro to Mount Kenya, about 180 miles directly north across the border; but right now, we're going in search of the carcass of a bull elephant that some fieldmen discovered just a few days ago. With us in the Defender are four Masai, clearly enjoying the novelty of motor travel. While the lucky few have bicycles, the bulk of the Masai have to go everywhere on foot, wearing makeshift shoes made of old motorbike tyres.

We find the elephant lying dead in a ditch, its tusks removed, but otherwise intact. As a culture that relies heavily on farming cattle, the Masai understand the killing of animals for use as food or clothing, but the senselessness of this act clearly dismays them, as well as myself.

"Elephant hunting was banned in 1989, but it still continues," says Lendiy, "Our resources are no match for those of the poachers." The ivory is eventually sold to places like Japan and China, where it remains a major status symbol.

Joseph Lendiy (pink shirt) studied in the US before returning to his Masai village; Kenyan anti-poachers mean business (above)

The next morning we say goodbye to Joseph Lendiy and begin the journey north. We're heading for Mount Kenya, but first we plan to stop off in Nairobi.

To sit behind the wheel of a contemporary Defender is to appreciate just how far the Land Rover brand has travelled in recent years. It's as strong and capable off-road as it is crude and unrefined on the terra firma, and it gives you a sense of confidence that few cars could match. Tackling terrain that requires complete concentration, the adrenalin pumping, you get a real sense of what has given this car such longevity and kudos. And it's not until you drive it in this kind of environment that you fully realise how wasted its talents are on UK tarmac, where the novelty of driving one quickly wears off and you find yourself wishing you were in a Range Rover. One thing's for sure – it's preferable to 95 per cent of the vehicles found on East African roads.

According to the latest statistics, there are 161 deaths per 10,000 vehicles in Tanzania each year. Even the worst 'developed' countries muster no more than five. To drive here is to witness a frightening cocktail of bad roads, bad driving and bad cars. And ambulances are a luxury found only in the heart of major cities.

It doesn't take us long to see the reality behind the statistics. On the main highway from Moshi to Arusha, we pass a small circle of people surrounding a body on the roadside. A mangled bike lies by his side and a pickup truck is in a ditch. Then, less than a mile later, we witness an almost identical scene. Two young lives have been lost in the last half-hour, but the atmosphere seems remarkably indifferent.

"Most people believe in 'God's will' ," explains Winnie Kiiru, our travelling companion from Born Free. "People accept that the person's time has come, which is why the reaction isn't as extreme as you might expect."

Scenes like this make it very difficult not to feel vulnerable. Driving here is an act of faith; you stick to a familiar path, hit the horn and hope for the best. Some of the overtaking is kamikaze and even our well-serviced vehicle has a worrying absence of rear seatbelts.

It's also impossible to escape the sheer poverty. On numerous occasions, we pass tiny metallic shacks that have been daubed with the phrase 'demolish order'. Needless to say, they are all inhabited by families. "The poverty is worse now than it was 10 years ago," says Kiiru. "There's no middle class, so there's no social ladder to climb. Young families today have very little hope." It's people caught in this cycle of deprivation that ultimately become poachers. But it's the middlemen, the ones that don't take the risks, who make the real profits from the trade.

'Tackling terrain that requires complete concentration, the adrenalin pumping, you get a real sense of what has given this car such longevity and kudos.'

GUINNESS
SHOP
SHOP
Hedex
61·90
60·90
DIESEL
47·50
KEROSENE
37·50
KAO 156B
UCHUMI BUTCHERY
Buy Kenyan Build Kenya
Rosy
Rosy
TOILET ROLL
Rosy®
TOILET ROLL

Despite these hardships, there's a buzz about the place that's rarely portrayed in the Western media. Kiiru agrees: "Although we appreciate their work, charities such as Live Aid tend to portray Africans as sad and helpless. We're really a very happy people – we don't have much, but we share what we do have."

It's dark by the time we arrive at the outskirts of Nairobi, and we're delayed by yet another accident. Peeking through the dust, it's possible to make out tiny wooden shops that service a community of truckers. The mood feels quite threatening – Kenya's capital boasts a potentially explosive mix of rich and poor – so it's a relief to finally reach the sanctuary of our hotel.

We're up early next day to complete our journey to Mount Kenya. The landscape to the north of Nairobi is dominated by pineapple fields, and the poverty is less acute here than south of the border. Although Kenya suffers from corruption, it has not had to endure the vacillations of former President Julius Nyerere's experimental socialism that blighted Tanzania's economy for a generation. The driving is just as bad, of course, but the Defender is up to the task. Going past another accident involving a cyclist, it's doubly reassuring to be cocooned in tough metal.

When we arrive at Mount Kenya, the lush Alpine vegetation comes as a surprise. For this part of the journey, we've been joined by two members of the Youth for Conservation (YFC) charity and Susie Weeks, who works for the Mount Kenya Trust. Weeks shows us a truly horrifying treasure chest of snares found on the mountain. Some are shocking in their barbarity.

"Wild game is poached and then sold as beef in the local butchers," she explains. "It's a big operation, but the people who actually do the poaching tend to be the poorest of the poor."

We take to a rock-strewn path and point the Land Rover up the mountain to meet up with two paramilitary members of the Kenya Wildlife Service. We are to join them on poaching patrol, and both men are armed. It's a particularly unnerving experience, given that neither of them speaks any English. As we make our way through the dense woodland, it isn't long before we find what we're looking for.

Lying across our path is a crude piece of wire, bent into the shape of a lasso. It's basic and indiscriminate. Just a few weeks ago, the rangers found an elephant that had lost its trunk in a snare like this. Unable to feed itself any more, the poor beast had had to be shot.

We stumble on further, only to discover the remains of a poached buffalo. Its stinking, rotting head has been dumped in the forest beside the traces of a campfire. "The poachers probably stopped to eat a quick meal here before carrying off their prey," says Peter Muigai of the YFC.

Having camped at 8000ft among the wildlife, but sadly not been able to permanently stop any poachers from their killing, we point the Defender back in the direction of Nairobi and our flight home. While East Africa has obvious problems, of which poaching is both an effect and a cause, it also has a vibrant, rich culture that is too often overlooked and unreported.

And it's no surprise that after a thousand miles of driving over some extremely trying terrain, my affection for the Defender has deepened. Its integrity of purpose is something that none of LR's modern range can match. Out here, it's as if the car itself has thrown off the fashionable, urban image, and is now free to express its doggedly determined qualities. Qualities that it is in Land Rover's interests to defend.

First printed in *Top Gear* magazine, February 2005

SMART TO THE ARCTIC

Taking a Smart ForTwo to meet Europe's Eskimos

Photographs TOM SALT

The Artic is an unlikely but hugely satisfying venue for the car enthusiast. In the winter months, you're likely stumble across a secret prototype in the midst of cold weather testing. Nearly all the European manufacturers use the freezing wastelands to test their new models in extreme conditions. The theory is simple: if a new hatchback can cope with minus 40 degress and a blizzard, then it can most likely cope with a supermarket car park.

The land of the midnight sun is also home to some of the world's finest driving schools. If you have a frozen lake and a tractor, you have the makings of a low grip circuit. There is no better way to learn the art of car control than to drive on snow and ice, and the laid-back Scandinavians make some of the finest tutors. Ex-Skoda rally driver, John Haughland, has a rally school in Norway and four-time world rally champion, Juha Kankkunen, runs a driving academy in Finland, for example.

The idea of taking a Smart to the Arctic had little to do with high performance driving or even winter testing. It was the kind of story that you do because you can. I've always had a taste for the absurd and the idea of taking a tiny city car 1500 miles north of the Arctic Circle seems so silly that it just had to be done. One wag even suggested that it already looked like an igloo.

A plan was hatched to take the Smart to meet the European equivalent of the North American Eskimos. In Lapland and beyond you'll find the Sami people, one of Europe's oldest indigenous populations. Theirs is a simple existence built around reindeer herding or fishing, but their traditions are under threat from the demands of a modern, commercial world. We were taking one endangered species, the slow-selling, loss-leading Smart, to meet another.

We flew to Helsinki, Finland, and then on to Rovaniemi, situated on the edge of the Arctic Circle. There we were met by a local guide with the Smart and a Mercedes M-class. The latter would carry the guide and serve as a support vehicle, should anything go wrong.

Ironically, the only vehicle that got stuck was the M-class. It sunk into a ditch on the edge of a frozen lake and we had to find a local farmer with a tractor to dig us out. It was a comical sight – a huge tractor trying to tow a large 4x4 out of a ditch while a tiny Smart looked on. And it was minus 30 degrees at the time.

Two years later, as I write these words, the future of the Smart brand looks less precarious than at perhaps any point in its history. The company has been rationalised and a new and much improved version of the ForTwo has been launched. The little car still polarises opinion – you either get it or you don't – but I've always been in the 'for' camp. The world needs interesting, small, fun and relatively inexpensive cars like the Smart.

The Smart's thermometer reads -30 degrees as we leave Rovaniemi. The road is clear and the busy buzz of the heater blends with the gentle throbbing of the tiny 698cc engine, while the studded tyres do battle with roads that could double as an ice rink.

To the scattered audience of moose, reindeer and huskies, we must be an extraordinary sight. A lanky Englishman is spearing across the Arctic in an odd red igloo, leaving behind the Lapp capital and the last remnants of civilisation.

Inside our tiny capsule, photographer Tom Salt and I are feeling cosy. The heater is just about keeping us warm, my iPod is set to 'easy listening', and we've a ready supply of reindeer salami. We might be a thousand miles from the Smart's natural, metropolitan habitat, but Daimler Chrysler's problem child has always felt strangely at home on the open road.

Ever since I drove Sir Stirling Moss's personal import in '98, I've been a fan of the Smart. It was a brand that was trying to offer something genuinely different in an over-congested market and, while the execution was flawed, it had great charm. Which other modern car is worthy of a place in New York's Museum of Modern Art?

But as many a chancer has found out, mere charm is not enough. Smart has haemorrhaged cash since day one and DC's bean counters have designed a Smart-shaped coffin. The Roadster and Roadster-Coupé have been killed off, the ForMore mini-SUV project has been terminated and although the ForTwo and ForFour continue for now, the future looks less than secure.

All of which, in my humble opinion, is an error and a shame. The car world needs the ForTwo more than it needs the Bugatti Veyron. It's the kind of car that naturally lends itself to madcap adventures, which is why I find myself here, in Finland, paying homage to the motoring equivalent of a prodigal son. If this is to be its last hurrah, it will be a mighty big shout.

The Smart is standard, save for studded snow tyres and an electric plug socket, which must be connected to the mains at night to keep the car functioning in temperatures that could dip as low as -50 degrees. Our guide says a typical temperature in early spring is a "comfortable" -20, but anything much below -30 is "genuinely cold." In such conditions, the Smart's glass roof grabs away any rise in temperature and the little heater is forced to work overtime.

More than 350km north of Rovaniemi, near the bedraggled town of Inari, we stumble across the Kakslauttanen husky farm. The guidebook promises real life huskies and tales of derring-do, so it seems worth a stop. The huskies are all present and correct – over 300 live on the end of a chain in an outdoor kennel – but the enterprise has more to do with giggling Yanks than authentic culture.

The first dog handler or 'musher' we meet speaks with a Welsh accent. Michael Colborn used to run a student bar in Bangor before he fell in love with a Finnish girl and moved to Inari. Maybe handling huskies is not too dissimilar to dealing with pissed-up students.

Colborn offers to attach a team of huskies to the Smart's tow hook, which seems like too good an opportunity to miss. My sextet of dogs is all female and led by a pair of lesbian hounds (seriously), but despite my best attempt at a Finnish-sounding 'mush', they refuse to move. Even Tom, who sleeps with a greyhound, can't get them to budge. Maybe they feel as silly as I look.

Before we leave, Colborn offers an interesting insight into the local culture. This area is, he explains, home to the Sami people, Europe's equivalent of the Inuit 'Eskimos'. "They number about 75,000 in Lapland and after decades of oppression, their culture's enjoying a revival," he says. "The language is taught in schools and there's even a Sami rap song."

Colborn points us in the direction of the Kaldoaivi reindeer farm, where I'm promised a 'genuine' experience. Getting there means venturing off-road but the Smart is surprisingly adept at crossing terrain that would trouble a hiker. Its

Sami costume is a sop to tourists (above); life on the Barings Sea (right)

electronic stability system has been improved in recent years to the extent that it can now be called a driver's aid, not a hindrance.

We're in a wooded area that feels like a special rally stage, but before I can shout "Call me Colin", my passenger shoots a disapproving look. After all, we're miles from anywhere, it's -25 outside, my mobile doesn't work and our 'survival gear' consists of a down-filled jumpsuit. Tom and I get on, but the thought of spending a night sharing body warmth doesn't appeal.

Eventually, the road reveals a wooden hut, several reindeer and a bloke in a garish costume. At a guess, I'd say Eric Hatta is 50 years-old and he has the wise, weathered face of a man who's spent his life outdoors. He's dressed in traditional Sami garb, with a garish jumper, reindeer-skin trousers and sieparat shoes. These boast upturned toes, like pixie boots, which can be bound to create makeshift skis. The outfit is a sop to the tourists, but it's also worn during Sami festivals.

For the past 10 years, Hatta and Kamu – his trusty reindeer – have been employed in the tourist trade, but his background reads like a Monty Python sketch. "My family has been reindeer herders for hundreds of years," he explains. "My grandfather, father and brothers are all herders." Today, the traditional kota tent has been replaced with a brick-built house and Hatta drives a Mazda 626, but he still reckons that the "Sami consciousness is growing."

The farm is tantalisingly close to the Russian border. All the guide books tell us it will take at least a couple of weeks to gather the requisite paperwork, but in the spirit of adventure, we decide to make a run for it. At sunset and much to the amusement of the Finnish border guards, a tiny red capsule arrives at the border post.

The scene could have been plucked from any Cold War movie. The Finnish border post is a few hundred metres in front of the Russian equivalent, in between which is a no-man's-land. Feeling a bit like Steve McQueen, I peer out into the gloom and just catch sight of the opposing camp. "We cross sometimes," says a friendly Finnish guard. "The fuel's cheaper over there." They pose for pictures with the Smart before turning us around. None shall pass.

After our near-Russian adventure, the hotel in Inari feels a bit of an anti-climax. Dinner consists, not surprisingly, of reindeer. South of the Arctic Circle, we flippantly call reindeers Rudolph, but up here, they provide food, clothing and income. Good reindeer steak is delicious, but the minced variety we're offered tonight tastes dangerously like doner kebab meat. I didn't come to Lapland to be reminded of student meals I'd much rather forget.

The handful of tourists who come to Inari care little for the food. The main attraction lies outside. Wander through this part of the world in the dead of night and you'll find hundreds of tourists, dressed like Michelin men, staring hopelessly at the sky in search of the northern lights. This phenomenon of the Arctic is not to be missed, which is why we, too, find ourselves in the middle of a frozen lake.

The Smart's computer reckons it's now -35 degrees and I'm not going to argue. Every time we step out of our pseudo-igloo, my nostrils crackle with frost and the icy air torments my lungs. Without the proper kit, you'd be lucky to survive more than a few minutes out here. Eventually, a little before 1am, God does his stuff and a vibrant arc of green light is thrown across the heavens. Tom busies himself with his Nikons before we dive back into the Smart. The car has become our equivalent of a Ray Mears tarpaulin shelter and roaring log fire.

We head north next morning towards the town of Utsjoki on the Norwegian border. The road was only built in 1957 and it cuts through a barren, icy wasteland that can have changed little in millennia. Crossing such terrain in a Smart feels faintly surreal and there's a repetitive crack-crackle from the tyres as they fight the ice.

In the UK, such treacherous conditions would carry a government health warning, but in Finland everyone just gets on with it. We spear along at 75mph in sixth gear, while the rear-end performs a rhythmical jiggle. The traffic is light and modest. And contrary to expectations, perhaps, we haven't seen an SUV for days.

It's late afternoon when we arrive in Utsjoki, which turns out to be no more than a gaggle of ugly buildings. There's little sign of life and the owner of the café seems surprised to have custom. For the price of a coffee and a piece of cake, she points us towards a genuine reindeer farm where, we're promised, real Sami are at work.

The road to the farm is framed by six-foot-high walls of snow, dwarfing the little Smart. Finally, we crest a brow to be confronted by the sight of 6000 reindeer circling in what looks like a maypole dance. We're introduced to Asko Lansman, who explains that the reindeer have been rounded up for branding before being released again. Lansman rides a snowmobile and buys his clothes on the Internet, but his family's lifestyle otherwise has changed little in centuries. In December, the beasts will be slaughtered and the yearly cycle will start over again.

It's dark when we cross the Norwegian border and, to the bemusement of the border guards, take the coast road east along the edge of the Barents Sea. There are Sami here too, but they live off the sea rather than reindeer. Apparently they even built the Vikings' fastest ships.

Sami consciousness is growing here too. "In the Fifties and Sixties, talk of the Sami culture was banned in schools, but that has changed," says Claus Petterson, the curator of a local museum. "People today are proud to be Sami."

And I'm proud of our little Smart. We're now about 700 miles north of the Arctic Circle and far removed from its natural habitat. But while no one would suggest that it's the ideal tool for an Arctic expedition, it's never let us down.

Seven years on from its launch, the Smart remains a genuinely different proposition, that appeals for its novelty, its attention to detail and its diminutive proportions. Time and evolution have rounded off some of the initial rough edges, and it's become well-liked by those who find it slots into their lifestyle.

Together, we've enjoyed an epic adventure, discovering a world and a people quite alien from the Europop norm. I just hope this is just another Smart story, and not an epitaph.

First printed in *Top Gear* magazine, February 2006

The Northern Lights are a cosmic phenomenon (below); our expedition to the Russian border is in vain (top)

'We're now about 700 miles north of the
Arctic Circle and far removed from the
Smart's natural habitat.'

MINI IN MOSCOW

Taking part in a semi-legal street race around the streets of Moscow

Photographs CHARLIE MAGEE

Ever since I studied Marx at school, I've been fascinated by the former Soviet bloc. I was left wide-eyed by the manner in which an economic theory could be used and brutally abused in the pursuit of absolute power. It still seems incredible to think that an academic working tirelessly in a London library could have been indirectly responsible for the deaths of tens of millions of people in the 20th century. Marx became, posthumously, the biggest mass murderer in history.

Growing up in Thatcher's Britain, it was also fascinating to imagine what life was really like behind the Iron Curtain. The popular image was of soup queues, Ladas and grey concrete tower blocks full of desperate people. We were told that this was a world without freedoms, where self-expression was banned and the state was all-consuming. This was Orwell's 1984 made real.

I was twelve when the Berlin Wall collapsed in 1989 – old enough to know what was going on, but not old enough to understand its true significance. It wasn't until 1995, when I was 18, that I finally visited the old East. I was touring Europe by train with three school friends and did a whistle-stop tour of Berlin, Prague, Budapest and Bucharest on my way to Istanbul. Six years after the Wall had fallen, there were tell-tale signs of western influence – mainly in the form of McDonald's restaurants – but the Trabants still vied with age-old trams for road space. These were countries in transition.

My first visit to Moscow came in 2003, when I was invited to witness the launch of the armoured Range Rover. This trip was as bizarre as it sounds. On our arrival we had a few hours to kill, so we visited Red Square and witnessed some of the old Soviet landmarks from the back seat of a Lada. Then, in the late afternoon, we were taken to an indoor tennis centre in the suburbs, which was to be the venue for the Range Rover's launch.

A meeting place for Moscow's new entrepreneurial class, the centre was run by an ex-member of the Russian special forces. An armoured vehicle was placed in the corner of a court as a motley crew gathered to watch. These were the bodyguards of Russia's new rich, men with scars upon their faces and guns on their belts. There were even bodyguards to guard the bodyguards.

From across the court a small figure in army fatigues approached the Range Rover. He unloaded eight shots from a Kalashnikov AK47 rifle into the side of the £240,000 car, stepped forwards and unloaded eight more shots from a Makarov pistol. We were then invited to inspect the damage.

The 'shooting of the Range Rover' was a surreal experience bettered only by my semi-legal street race around Moscow a year later. How I did not end up in a Russian jail, I'll never know.

С091НТ 97
RUS

The pool ball has a deeper meaning; Moscow State University boasts Stalinesque architecture and 40,000 undergrads

In the UK, street races are normally the preserve of spotted oiks in Vauxhall Novas, pedalling like fury around an ugly urban centre. The kind of event, in other words, that manufacturers would rather not be associated with. But in Russia, more relaxed laws, easily bribed policemen and a newfound hedonism create an atmosphere that's ripe for some old-fashioned tomfoolery. BMW has even started getting in on the act in Moscow ...

It's 10pm on Saturday. I find myself signing on as a competitor in the MINI Moscow Marathon, a carefully-choreographed street race organised by BMW Russia. Billed as a social jamboree cum motorsports event, the Marathon has attracted 25 racers in a variety of MINIs. There are a couple of examples of the original Mini, but my chosen charge is a Works Cooper S, the most powerful of all the 'official' MINIs.

The profile of my fellow competitors is a surprise. In Russia, MINIs aren't as well-priced as they are here. Even the cheapest model costs over £20k and a Cooper S will be closer to £30k. "We only sold 150 here last year," explains Elena Kravets, MINI's marketing guru. "People in Russia like to express their wealth and success by owning a big car. They normally buy a MINI as a third car, often for their daughters." That also explains why rear parking sensors are fitted as standard, apparently. "Girls don't know how to park," Elena says.

As if to illustrate her point, Kravets introduces me to Maria Kitaeva, who is giggling excitedly behind the wheel of her Cooper S. "My parents bought it for me for my last birthday present," says the 20 year-old, a student at the University of International Relations. But aren't her parents concerned that she's taking part in a street race? "Maybe they don't know too much about it," she says with a grin.

I'm handed a bag of clues that includes a pool ball, a chocolate dinosaur and a model car. I've been teamed with a Russian journalist, Igor Shein, and we must visit six locations and perform a variety of tasks. Each section will be timed so the speed of our driving, even in the city, will be of crucial importance.

At about 10:30pm the flag drops and we explode into the Moscow traffic. The John Cooper Works kit for the Cooper S costs around £3500 in the UK and increases the MINI's power output to 200bhp. It's the quickest car here, but I'm nervous about exploiting its potential in a busy city centre. And my concerns are exacerbated when I spot a MINI receiving Police attention within 500 yards of the start. "Don't worry," says Shein, "the fines are normally only about 100 Roubles (£2)."

Feeling far from reassured, I arrive at the first control stop, a Citibank on Tverskaja, Moscow's equivalent of Oxford Street. I'm tasked with estimating the number of gold bars in a safe and after guessing correctly, I receive a bonus score and the location of the next control. We speed southwest past Red Square and I can't help wondering what Lenin would think of all this. "I suspect he'll be turning in his mausoleum," Shein says with a laugh.

A rival exits the 'pit lane'; 'driving like an Englishman' means finishing last; Minis in Red Square at 4am (overleaf)

Motoring in Moscow today is very different from the '80s cliché. LADAs still exist, but they now jostle for road space with Mercedes, BMWs and Range Rovers. A local casino is even offering a £280k Maybach as a prize. The scene is extremely ostentatious, and everyone drives like they're fleeing the KGB.

My second and third tasks involve potting the pool ball (I miss) and dressing a female mannequin while blindfolded (no problem). Then it's back across the city in search of a shooting range. En route I spot my first horse of the evening. A huge brown mare is wandering across a busy backstreet carrying a helmet-less rider. "You can hire them for about 100 Roubles an hour," says Shein, casually. "They're quite popular."

The range turns out to be no more than a bar with a shooting gallery and I'm asked to fire a pistol at a cartoon figure. Unfortunately, the instructions are in Russian and I fail to understand the warning about kickback. I miss the target and leave the bar with a black eye. Not good.

At 11:30pm I'm stopped by the Police for the first time. No doubt intrigued by the presence of a racing number on the side of my MINI, they want to see all my documents before I'm allowed to go. I continue until I'm stopped again. And again. Each time we go through the same process and each time I'm sent on my way. "They're disappointed that you have the correct documents," claims Shein, "they saw the car and anticipated a big pay day."

We arrive too late to complete the final task and are led to the exclusive Zima nightclub, where the winners will be presented with their trophy. It's packed with people wearing ludicrous clothes, and parked on the road outside are a Ferrari 360, a Bentley Arnage and a fleet of S-Class Mercedes.

Kitaeva finished second and is bubbling with enthusiasm. "I got stopped by a Policeman for crossing the road's centre line," she explains. "But I told him to hurry up because I was in a race. I paid him 100 Roubles and he asked what the prize was. Apparently, he'd already stopped someone else." Nineteen year-old Anna Tienka had only been chased by her father. "My dad was worried about me, so he tried to follow me in his Jeep," she says. "But I soon lost him."

Nobody will confirm my position, but I definitely didn't make the top three and rumour has it I came dead last. "You drove like an Englishman," reckons Kitaeva. "You were always thinking about the rules and being sensible. Russians don't drive like that." A six-foot blonde named Katya is equally unimpressed – "I bet on you to win," she explains at the finish. "I thought you looked fast."

It's a bizarre end to an extraordinary event. I've just taken part in a semi-legal street race, sanctioned by BMW and held in the heart of Moscow. Saturday nights don't get any better than this.

First printed in *The Sunday Times*, 9th May 2004

13
E208EO 62
RUS

200-02-14
ПЕРЕХОД
К 969 ЕЕ 97 RUS
В 407 МР 77

LAMBORGHINI TO THE FAROE ISLANDS

How far would you go to drive a supercar?

Photographs TOM SALT

I was sitting at my desk one afternoon when the phone rang. It was Tom Salt, who is both a friend and one of the world's best automotive photographers. "I want to go to the Faroe Islands," he said, "are you up for it?" This was one of life's more surreal moments.

In the back of my brain I recalled that the Faroes once embarrassed Scotland at football, but that's about all I could remember. To my shame, I didn't even know where they are. "They're in the north Atlantic," explained Tom, "about half-way between Scotland and Iceland. They're supposed to be beautiful."

We did some research and realised that there was no easy route to the Faroes. If we wanted to go, we'd have to drive to Aberdeen in Scotland, catch an overnight ferry to the Shetlands Isles, spend a few hours there and then go overnight again to the Faroes. We'd spend three days there and repeat the process in reverse. In total, we'd be away for about ten days but if the Islands were as beautiful as Tom thought, then it would be worth it.

I dreamt up a simple tag line for the story: "How far would you go to drive a supercar?" and offered it to the UK's biggest selling car magazine, Top Gear. *It is one of the great pleasures of this job that if a couple of big publications are willing to back your crazy idea, then you can pretty much do anything you want. To my delight, the magazine's editor, Michael Harvey, said he'd take the story. The race was on to find the right car.*

My first choice was the new Porsche 997 (911) Turbo. The 911 has always been billed as the consummate everyday, long distance supercar and the turbo is its ultimate expression. Sadly, the UK press office had only one car available and it was in demand. They weren't keen on the idea of lending it to us for 10 days and over 2000 miles.

"We've sold them all," said the PR man "we don't need the publicity." This seemed a strange attitude – I've always thought that stories about 911 Turbos are all about selling Boxsters to aspirational city-types.

Undeterred, I called Lamborghini and asked for a Gallardo roadster. I was in luck. They had an Italian registered car that was due to go back to the factory in Sant' Agata, but they could delay its return. We were on.

With hindsight, I think the Lamborghini was a far better choice. The 911 is a magnificent car, but it is now a ubiquitous sight and lacks the pure theatre of a Gallardo. It is impossible to drive a Lamborghini without drawing attention to yourself and, for the purposes of this story, attention was what we craved.

The Faroes exceeded our expectations. We knew the scenery would be stunning, but we didn't expect the people to be so friendly, or the girls to be so beautiful. Sometimes the best stories are born of the silliest ideas.

CY 001GX

Jakup Borg once had a trial with Liverpool FC; the perfect British breakfast – a fry-up and *The Sun* newspaper

"So, why have you brought a Lamborghini to the Faroe Islands?" asks the man in the sober grey suit. "I wanted to come somewhere with dramatic scenery and great roads," I explain. "To a place where there are no speed cameras or petty bureaucracy." The man looks a little concerned and photographer Salt intervenes. "Alistair," he says, "let me introduce you to the Faroes Minister for Transport."

It is an inauspicious start. My new-found friend, Bjarni Djurholm, turns out also to be the Minister for Trade and Industry and, for the moment at least, the acting Prime Minister. I arrived in the Faroe Islands less than two hours ago and I've already embarrassed myself.

Djurholm admits to being a Lamborghini fan and wants a ride in the car. We trundle out of town as I wonder whether to break the modest, 80km/h speed limit. At this speed, in fourth gear, the Gallardo Spyder burbles away contentedly, but it feels no more exciting than a Focus.

"I think you should overtake the car in front," says Mr Djurholm, proving that laws are there to be broken, especially if you've made them yourself. I shift to second, flex my right foot and the V10 takes a lug of fuel. At full throttle, the Gallardo makes a noise that's devilishly naughty. While Ferrari's F430 proffers a high-pitched, F1-mimicking scream, the Lambo plays a symphony of trumpets. "It's even better than I imagined," says my passenger.

We make a U-turn at the top of a hill and then sprint back to Tórshavn, the capital of the Faroes. "I used to have a picture of a Lamborghini as a boy," says the acting Prime Minister between spurts of acceleration. "This is like a dream." His childish enthusiasm is shared by his electorate: a crowd has gathered to greet our return and a dozen camera phones are thrust into action.

The Islands are far from poor – Djurholm reckons the standard of living is higher than that in the UK – but prohibitive car tax excludes the exotic. No one can ever remember a Lamborghini visiting these shores before, which is why our

'The scenery in the Faroe Islands is different to that of northern Scotland or the Shetland Isles. It's much more aggressive, with steep gradients and jagged coastlines, as if some other-worldly being has nibbled at giant chunks of earth and left the rest to rot.'

arrival has been akin to that of Dr Livingstone – "*Top Gear*, I presume." The tv show is hugely popular here and our visit made headline news in one of the local newspapers. Their only disappointment is that I'm not Clarkson (who is soon to own a Gallardo), Hammond or May.

Situated halfway between Scotland and Iceland in the middle of the North Atlantic, the Faroe Islands are an extraordinary place. They're home to just 48,000 people but they boast their own language and their own bank notes. Officially, the Islands are part of the Kingdom of Denmark but their Parliament has autonomy over local issues.

For a place of such natural beauty, the Faroes receive little attention. Part of the problem is their remote location. We left London on Friday, drove to Perth and then on to Aberdeen, where we caught an overnight ferry to the Shetlands. "Is that Lamborghini real?" asked a ferryman. "We thought it might have been one of them replicas."

After eight hours in the Shetlands we caught a second and surprisingly plush ferry to the Faroes.

Next year, the local Smyril Line will open a direct ferry route from Scotland, which will make life easier. There are plenty of flights, but a Gallardo might fall foul of hand baggage restrictions.

As a long-distance tool, the Lambo is surprisingly capable. Gone are the days when it was the automotive equivalent of a poster-boy dunderhead – pretty but useless. The purists might bemoan the company's German ownership but there can be no denying that it has resulted in a much better Lamborghini. Everything works.

After the Shetlands – a place so grey it looks like it's been desaturated – the Faroes adds a welcome dash of colour. Quaint wooden buildings are dotted around Tórshavn's pretty harbour and many boast roofs made of turf. "When we want to cut the grass, we just throw up a couple of sheep," says a local, half-joking. The vibe is laidback and surprisingly cool – very Scandinavian.

The local jet-wash is run by Jakup Borg, who plays in midfield for the Faroes football team. "I had a month-long trial with Liverpool in 1998," he says. "I've also played for the Faroes against Germany but Michael Ballack wouldn't swap shirts, his attitude was, 'who are you?'"

Like many of the Faroese we've met, Borg seems content. "There's no crime," he says. "Tórshavn is a good place to be – there are eight bars and four nightclubs – but some of the other communities feel like they're stuck in the Sixties or Seventies."

Our Lamborghini has been disparagingly described as a 'footballer's car', but this is to do it a disservice. Sitting soaking on the garage floor, it rekindles memories of the original Countach, before it was polluted by wings and scoops. It's a refreshingly pure design that works well from every angle, hood up or down.

But such beauty is not achieved without compromise and Borg laughs out loud when I open the boot. The cubby in the nose is so small that my luggage for a week's trip has been reduced to two tatty carrier bags. From day three onwards, I'll be forced to wear my underpants inside out.

After posing for an inevitable picture, we leave the affable Borg to his labour and head for the hills. The scenery in the Faroe Islands is different to that of northern Scotland or the Shetland Islands. It's much more aggressive, with steep gradients and jagged coastlines, as if some other-worldly being has nibbled at giant chunks of earth and left the rest to rot.

In the early '90s the Faroes government built tunnels that link most of the 18 islands. Most traffic now takes the underground route which has left some of the more dramatic roads deserted. The one that runs northwest from Tórshavn is seminal. Stretching for some 20km, it criss-crosses the hillside before plunging down the valley. Wide and beautifully surfaced, it's supercar nirvana.

With the roof down, the sonorous cry of the 520bhp, 5.0-litre V10 is much more accessible.

I slot-shift to second and give it the beans. The Gallardo scoops itself up and flings itself at the horizon. The pub-bore stats – 0-60mph takes just 4.3secs and a top whack of 195mph – tell only part of the tale. The throttle response is angry and immediate and the manual 'box hops from cog to-cog with a metallic ping that's hugely emotive.

At high speed, the Alcantara steering wheel chats like an adolescent on a first date, while the suspension flatters the bumpy surface. My fears that the chop-top Gallardo would be no more than a boulevard playboy are dispatched in an instant. So much of the coupés grace and favour has been retained, but now it's been given a more earthy quality. You interact with this car like no Lamborghini before it.

This road leads to the tiny communities that line the northern coastline and on day two we pay them a visit. Tiny gaggles of grass-roofed houses, often no more than 20, cling to the seashore. Most of these hamlets possess a church but nothing else. "We have to travel half-an-hour for milk," explains a resident of Gjógv. Parked beside these houses, the Lamborghini has never looked more incongruous and its soundtrack makes me feel self-conscious.

Given the paucity of entertainment and the relative affluence of the population, it's no surprise to discover a buoyant car culture. "A car in the Faroe Islands is either transport from a to b or a flat in which you socialise," Djurholm tells me. "In small communities, there is nowhere to meet." At night, local youths lap the streets of Tórshavn in a steady procession.

The cruisers are magnetically drawn to the Lamborghini. Word has spread of where we're staying and each night our hotel is besieged by groups of young people, desperate to pose by our toy. Even the local police turn up for a gawp and they're joined by a group of bikers. "In the Faroes motorbike tax is not so high and even a 20 year-old can have a superbike," says Jakup Djurhuvs. "One of our friends was killed last week, but we do not learn." I'm challenged to a race but think better of it.

For some locals, this passion for all things automotive has become an obsession. On day three, we're introduced to Sofus Hansen, nicknamed Fuzzy. The Faroes' only car-builder operates out of a tiny garage beneath his house. Fuzzy earns a decent living spray painting cars but bespoke coachwork is his primary art. A restyled Harley sits beside a Porsche 928 that's been crossed with a Peugeot 407. The results may not be to all tastes, but there's no doubting the craftsmanship. "People think I'm a crazy playboy," he says.

Fuzzy also has a niece. Ever since we arrived, we've been noticing the strength of the Faroese gene pool and Barbara Carlsen is its crowning glory. She works in the mayor's office in Tórshavn but has achieved local fame by singing in a gospel choir. "The Faroes is boring," she complains as she inspects the Gallardo, "there's nothing here to do." I nod pathetically. Faced with exceptional beauty, I've forgotten how to speak.

Our meeting proves a fitting climax to what has been a fascinating few days. Like Barbara, the Faroes are small but beautifully formed.

We left London a week ago not sure what we'd find. There was a danger that we'd be bored by the Faroes and irritated by the Gallardo's impracticality, but both have exceeded our expectations. The Faroe Islands probably aren't the most exciting place in which to grow up, but they're a great place to visit and the roads are terrific.

The baby Lamborghini has also sustained my interest. The Gallardo is a brilliantly engineered tool that doesn't rely on its supermodel looks to seduce. Home is seven hundred miles away, and I'm looking forward to every one.

First printed in *Top Gear* magazine, December 2006

Barbara 'Barbie' Carlsen reveals the strength of the Faroese gene pool; Lamborghini looks stunning with the roof up or down

MERCEDES TO THE MILLE MIGLIA

Taking one SLR to meet another at the 2005 Mille Miglia

Photographs ANTON WATTS

I first drove the Mercedes SLR back in 2000, when it was still known as the 'Vision' concept. Such events happen several times a year in the automotive world. A manufacturer invites a select group of journalists to a foreign (sunny) clime to drive a show car. Invariably, such drives are no more than a 30mph cruise along a closed section of road, while the engineer in the passenger seat points out that this is "only a concept."

These events are really no more than a means of equiring some nice photographs of the car away from a motorshow stand. Any driving impressions are entirely fatuous, but that has never stopped some of the less scrupulous car magazines from claiming an "exclusive first drive" of a car that won't be launched for several years.

That original Vision SLR 'drive' in Majorca followed the traditional formula. It told me nothing about how Mercedes' new supercar would perform, but I did learn that the car would be pure theatre. If the show-car looks could be carried over from concept to production, then the SLR would turn heads like no other. This was a supercar that succeeded in looking super.

The production car that emerged four years later had indeed changed little from that original concept. It was ridiculously expensive (over £300k) but it looked fabulous and had the instant credibility of being built by McLaren. The British company is responsible for Mercedes' efforts in Formula One and in the '90s had built the F1, arguably the most beautifully crafted supercar of all time.

The modern SLR could also claim a tenuous association with the original SLR. The latter was a race car built to help Stirling Moss win the most fearsome road race of them all, the Mille Miglia. When, in 2005, Moss celebrated the 50th anniversary of his most famous triumph, it seemed like the ideal opportunity to take the new SLR to meet the original. A 3000 mile jaunt from London to southern Italy and back would reveal much about the new SLR, and even more about Moss' stupendous achievement.

In today's sanitised world, it is often easy to forget just how dangerous motor racing used to be. At the time of writing, no-one has been killed or even seriously injured in Formula One for thirteen years, but when Moss was racing, three or four men would perish each year. Death was an occupational hazard; an inevitable fact of life. Moss himself was almost killed when he crashed at the Goodwood Circuit in 1962, a crash that would end his career.

Talking to Stirling, peering into the cockpit of the '722' SLR and driving the roads on which he averaged almost 100mph for 10 hours, it was impossible not to be in awe of his achievements. Even Moss himself couldn't quite believe what he had done.

722

Original SLR was built for racing and has a simple, brutal beauty; the modern-day Mille is a car spotter's nirvana

Stirling Moss didn't much care for the Mille Miglia. "I didn't like it at all," he exclaims in the crisp, old English accent that's become his trademark. "God, no ... it was the only race I ever did that frightened me because I knew that I couldn't learn a thousand miles of road. It wasn't my idea of a good time, it was too dangerous."

His candor raises a smile. Moss is now 75 years-old, and his thoughts, comments, and aspirations are from a different age. There's no PR spin, just an honest insight into the background to one of motorsport's greatest-ever drives.

At 7:22am on May 1, 1955, Moss left Brescia at the wheel of a Mercedes-Benz 300SLR with journalist Denis Jenkinson for company. Ten hours, seven minutes, and 48 seconds later, the Mercedes returned to this modest Italian town with 1000 miles on the clock. On public roads, closed for the occasion, Moss had achieved an average speed of 97.9mph.

After 50 years, Moss and the SLR are back in Brescia to celebrate the anniversary of their epic performance. The original Mille Miglia was banned in 1957 after a tragic accident left 12 dead, but the concept was revived in 1977 as a classic-car run. Low speed timed sections provide a competitive element for those who care, but for most of the 375 entrants, the retrospective Mille Miglia is a 1000-mile jaunt through some of God's most beautiful countryside.

Only cars built for the event's heyday – 1927-1957 – are entitled to enter, and this year's list of participants reads like a motorsport who's who. The SLR will be kept company by Jaguar D-Types, Ferraris, Bentleys, Porsches, and Chryslers.

Advancing years will limit Moss's role to a celebratory sprint from the start line. He'll then hand over the SLR to veteran sports car ace Jochen Mass, who will complete the course.

Mercedes would like you to think that my choice of car is a direct descendant of the all-conquering '722.' But while the Mercedes SLR McLaren shares a name with the 1955 original, it's built to a different brief. The contemporary SLR is billed as the ultimate Grand Tourer, mixing Mercedes civility with McLaren grunt and panache. A 2000-mile jaunt from London to the end of the Mille Miglia should prove whether this car is worthy of its hallowed name and inflated price tag.

The original SLR is waiting for us in the town center and is a picture of elegant aggression. Mercedes's desire for a straight-eight engine configuration made for an exceptionally long wheelbase, but the 3.0-litre's output of 290 horsepower was enough to propel the car beyond 170mph.

Every vantage point is cherished; this cigar will probably take 1000 miles to smoke

"It's a real man's car," says Moss, as we peek into the contorted cockpit. "You don't mince around with the SLR. It's a difficult car to drive but it's responsive to the throttle. You use the steering to present the car to the corner and then use the throttle to make it do what you want."

Most old racing cars frighten at a standstill, and 722 is no exception. There are no rollcages or seatbelts, and a 100-gallon fuel tank is located directly behind the driver. Jenkinson recalls being doused with fuel for 15 miles after leaving Rome, but electing not to tell his driver. "Fire was our biggest fear," says Moss today, "and that's why we decided not to wear seatbelts. I'd seen a man die at Sebring because he was trapped in the car, and that image stayed with me."

It's late evening before the cars exit Brescia and begin the relatively short hop to an overnight stay in Ferrara. Next morning, we leave for Rome. For the first hour, our 21st-century SLR runs in convoy with a 300SL Gullwing and a Ferrari 250 TDF. The regulations stipulate that the competitors must abide by the rules of the road – but this is Italy, and anything goes. We funnel in and out of traffic, making three lanes instead of two, and all the while we're accompanied by police outriders, sirens flashing.

The SLR's performance can encourage delirium. The 5.4-litre supercharged V8 develops a headline-grabbing 617 horsepower at 6500rpm, but it's the 575 poundfeet of torque available at 3250rpm that's the real clue to this car's performance. To summon enough thrust to overtake a stream of traffic, you don't so much prod the throttle as to gently curl a right toe. Concentration and delicacy are the prerequisites of smooth, rapid progress.

The drive out from London through France, Belgium, Germany, and the Swiss Alps had been instructive. For all its electric steering-wheel adjustment and automatic gearbox, the SLR isn't an easy car to drive. It's stiff and pointy like no other Merc, and the slightest tweak of the steering prompts an instantaneous response – sneeze and you could end up in another state.

It also takes time to acclimatise to the ceramic disc braking system. By opting for a floor-hinged pedal (the throttle is conventional), Mercedes has denied the controls a consistency of response. While the brakes' ultimate stopping power can't be questioned, it's difficult to modulate their impact. Miles and familiarity alleviates the problem, but it never fully goes away.

At least the brakes are better than those of the original SLR, which relied on drum technology. "They were terrible," Moss remembers, "but brakes exist for two reasons–to slow the car down and to give the driver confidence. I used them more to position the car than to slow it down–if we'd had air brakes, I don't think we'd

'The SLR's performance can encourage delirium.'

RX54 AEA

'On the road, this car is pure theatre.'

Leaving Rome in a 1955 300SL Gullwing (top left); why are you looking at me? Helmets come in all shapes and sizes

At least the brakes are better than those of the original SLR, which relied on drum technology. "They were terrible," Moss remembers, "but brakes exist for two reasons – to slow the car down and to give the driver confidence. I used them more to position the car than to slow it down – if we'd had air brakes, I don't think we'd have been as fast."

We arrive in San Marino, and the extravagance of my charge, coupled with some Latino insouciance, lends me access to a closed section of city streets. While the route of the contemporary Mille Miglia mimics that of the original, it also includes a series of tours through Rome, Florence, Modena, and Cremona.

The cobbled streets are absurdly narrow, and there's only a couple of inches clearance on either side of the McLaren's extravagant wing mirrors. Scratching the car here, on a stray postcard stand, would not be clever. I navigate the streets at little more than walking pace, but this at least affords me the opportunity to study the crowd's reaction.

There are plenty of people who think the SLR shape has been overcooked and that it lacks the elegance of simplicity. There's some validity in this, but on the road, this car is pure theatre. To cruise to a halt and throw open the scissor doors is to provoke spontaneous cries of appreciation. This car looks and sounds expensive, which is just as well, given that it costs $455,500.

Out of the city and on toward Rome. The roads open up here, and I find myself leaning harder on the loud pedal. McLaren's engineers have done a magnificent job of tuning this car's acoustics. On full throttle, the deep melodic roar is reminiscent of a Can Am racer, and it's worth using the gearbox's sequential facility just to keep it singing above 4000rpm.

There are times on these roads when I touch 130mph, but this does no more than confirm the magnificence of Moss's achievement. Sir Stirling benefited from closed roads and Jenks's elaborate pace notes, but this still can't explain how he was able to sustain 170mph speeds for long periods on blacktop that causes the modern SLR to tramline badly.

Even Moss thinks he must've been mad. "When I think that I averaged nearly 98mph, including three mountain passes, I can't quite believe it," he says. "I must have been very brave when I was younger." At one point, traveling at 170mph, the duo took off over a crest and flew for 200 feet. "I saw Jenks tugging on his beard, so I knew we were in trouble," says Moss, "but we landed safely." On another occasion, the pair overtook a twin-engine plane that was filming the event.

The start of leg three is in Rome, and I swap the SLR for a 1955 300SL.

The SLR draws a crowd wherever it goes; the 300SL enters Florence

Borrowed from the Mercedes museum in Stuttgart, this immaculate Gullwing coupé is worth around $400,000 and has the words "don't crash me" written in invisible ink on its doors. We leave Rome and head for Tuscany with the SL's 215 horsepower engine singing merrily in front of my toes. The Gullwing needs careful handling – the rear suspension is crude and the steering weights-up alarmingly through quick corners, but the car that was the darling of Hollywood in the 1950s still conjures a huge sense of occasion. It's almost a shame when I return to the SLR for the afternoon session.

By early evening, I've completed the legendary Futa mountain pass and am speeding through Bologna and on toward Modena. I tag along behind a police car as we blast through red lights, sprint down bus lanes, and dart through traffic. I have no genuine right to do so, but the local police take a laissez-faire attitude to glamorous wheels.

We're making swift progress but nothing like the kind of progress Moss was making. Jenkinson recorded that, "in the cramped and confined space of our traveling hothouse and bath of filth and perspiration," they traversed the center of Florence at 120-130mph and entered Bologna at an incredible 150mph. Moss had been driving flat out for more than nine hours when he averaged 123mph on the final stretch from Cremona to Brescia, and he was still traveling at more than 100mph as he crossed the finish line, wondering whether he'd won.

That final stretch, on wide-open, flowing roads, offers scope for reflection. The contemporary SLR has significant flaws – the brakes remain a problem, the steering could use more feel, and the interior is awash with poor detailing and questionable plastics. But for all its faults, the SLR still has a sense of drama that's difficult to resist.

The noise is sensational, and time behind the wheel has bred confidence in the chassis; where once it felt nervous, it now feels responsive and agile. The fusion between McLaren and Mercedes also feels better resolved than it did on first acquaintance. This is a supercar you could use everyday, but it also succeeds in feeling dramatically different from a standard AMG.

I imagined what it must've been like 50 years ago when 10 million people lined a thousand miles of road to watch a plucky young Brit and his Mercedes explore the limits of human endeavor. We will never see its like again.

First printed in *Motor Trend* magazine, August 2005

200MPH IN GERMANY

Breaking 200mph on the public road — and it's all perfectly legal

Photographs TOM SALT

Four days before I was due to take to the autobahn at the wheel of a Brabus EV12, the following email dropped into my inbox:

*"Ok. i know i do not have to say this but i'm gonna say it anyway: you are under no circumstances to do anything f*cked up or stupid. this silly little feature ain't worth the death of my favorite limey. if you die, i'll haunt yer ghost till it's dead too. have fun, be safe." lb*

'lb' was Les Bidrawn, editor of European Car, *the magazine that had commissioned the feature. Les is one of life's characters – he drinks Red Bull for breakfast and his choice of language is eccentric and often colourful. But he cares passionately about his job and his email was heart-felt and appreciated.*

Les knew that I intended to attempt 200mph on a stretch of German autobahn. For his US-based readers, this was an exotic story – taking the world's fastest sedan to its limit on a public highway without the threat of prosecution. But it also carried an element of risk. With every mile per hour gained, the forces acting on a car are tripled. If anything were to go wrong in northern Germany, they'd be picking up the pieces in Holland.

Many so-called experts will tell you that such enterprises are stupid, that the driver is a threat to society and should be locked up. In the UK, a high profile campaign dictates that 'speed kills.' But this denies an important truth. It is not speed that kills per se, but inappropriate speed. Doing 70mph in heavy traffic in the rain is almost certainly more dangerous than doing 120mph on a clear read in perfect visibility.

When Richard Hammond, a presenter of the hugely popular Top Gear *TV show had a near-fatal crash at 300mph while driving a jet car, 'experts' lined up to criticise his actions. We were told that Hammond had been taking an unnecessary risk and that driving at such speeds was inherently unsafe. Few in authority were willing to accept that what had happened was an accident, pure and simple.*

Hammond had been driving a car designed to do 300mph, on a private airfield and with medical staff in attendance. The car had been developed to withstand an accident at very high speed and Hammond wore the best helmet available. These precautions helped ensure that he made a full recovery, and the subsequent investigation into the crash cleared those involved of any significant wrongdoing. It was an accident.

I also took precautions before embarking on my 200mph adventure. On the German autobahn that morning, the traffic was sparse, the car was fit for purpose, and I have been trained to drive at high speed. Those three factors helped us manage the risk and turn a potentially dangerous enterprise into something that was relatively easy to achieve. Les got his story, and I got a thoroughly exhilarating experience.

BOT 06070

It's 4:30am in northern Germany and I'm parked in a rest area on the A31 autobahn. Dormant trucks fill the parking bays, their drivers snatching some sleep before heading north for the coast. At my side, the Brabus EV12 is ticking gently, recovering from one exertion and preparing for another.

Despite the early hour, its driver is awake ... very awake. I slept little last night in anticipation of this morning's activities. The keys in my hand give life to the fastest sedan in the world, a car that has been independently tested at 350km/h, or 217mph to you and me. That speed was achieved on the Nardo test track in Italy and I won't be trying to match it this morning. But I will be attempting to top 200mph on a two-lane highway littered with weary truckers.

The autobahnen were one of the few positive legacies of Germany's Nazi regime. Adolf Hitler had them built so the German population could see and appreciate the Fatherland. They were derestricted then and they are derestricted now. Put simply, you can drive as fast as your car, or your common sense, will allow. They're a wonderful dose of anarchy in a country obsessed with rules and regulations.

The engine starts on the first turn of a familiar E-Class key. Mercedes' ubiquitous biturbo V12 has been stroked by Brabus so that it now displaces 6.3-litres. Surgically implanted into the E-Class engine bay, it develops 640bhp at 5100rpm and an extraordinary 757lb-ft of torque at just 1750rpm. Pause and consider those figures for a moment. Even the much-vaunted SLR McLaren musters only 626bhp and 576lb-ft. Whichever way you look at it, the Brabus' output could properly be described as ample.

But the engine isn't loud, not even slightly. "Our customers want the civility of an E200 with the performance of a racecar," says Brabus PR guru, Sven Gramm, who's bravely come along for the ride. That also helps to explain why this car is painted black and wears only the minimum of aerodynamic addenda. Only a carbon-fiber front chin spoiler, subtle side skirts, a trunk lip spoiler and a tiny rear diffuser differentiate this car from a standard EClass. "We spent four days in the wind tunnel," says Gramm. "Don't worry, it won't take off." I hope he's right.

On to the autobahn and my first ginger mile in a car worth the not insignificant sum of $425,000. The steering system was lifted from a CLS because it's marginally more responsive and offers better feedback than the E-Class helm. The Bilstein suspension system is all new and was developed specifically for this car. "Mercedes' Airmatic system can't cope above 200mph," says Gramm, "because it can't react fast enough." Apparently, one of the Brabus test drivers had "a huge moment" while testing an Airmatic car on the open road. Nice.

Several things are immediately obvious. This car is subtle to the point of obscurity. As we drift past trucks at more than 100mph, nobody gives us a second glance. Maybe they're used to seeing Brabus in this part of the world (we're only a few miles from the factory), or maybe they think we're in a diesel. "Everybody knows the E-Class is a taxi," says Gramm with a grin. Right now, I really wish this car wasn't so discreet – if I'm going to pass people at 200mph, I'd rather they knew I was there.

The second thing to note is that for all its civility, this car is monstrously rapid. I've been fortunate enough to drive some mighty quick road and racecars, but few have ever snapped my head back with such determined force. The effect is so exaggerated that after a few miles I begin to feel like a cartoon character. For the record, this car will hit 200km/h (124mph) from rest in 11.7 seconds and 300km/h (186mph) in 30.6, but raw figures will never do justice to the sensation of brutal, animalistic thrust.

Not so long ago, this stretch of highway was the road to nowhere. It stopped so abruptly that few people ever bothered to use it and it became Brabus' own private playground. Recently, though, it's been extended and has become more popular. I'm beginning to think that it's too busy and that we've missed our chance, when Gramm motions me forward. "This is a good stretch," he says, "not so many bumps."

I push hard on the throttle and the automatic gearbox searches for a lower ratio. This is the five-speed 'box from the Maybach, but it's been modified and strengthened by Brabus. Everything seems so absurdly easy; you just extend

'It's 4:30am in northern Germany and I'm parked in a rest area on the A31 autobahn . At my side, the Brabus EV12 is ticking gent recovering from one exertion and preparing for another.'

BRABUS
BOT 06070

'... let this 4453-pound projectile suck in the horizon.'

SRS
AIRBAG
BRABUS
EV12

V12

'After what I've just experienced, 150mph feels pedestrian and I have to talk myself down to a more modest speed. The adrenalin is still pumping.'

a right toe, take a quarter-to-three grip on the wheel and let this 4453-pound projectile suck in the horizon. It's as astonishing as it is intoxicating.

At 130mph, all is calm, civilized. Only the relative speed of the trucks gives any indication that we're already traveling at twice the US legal limit. The Brabus seems so relaxed that it's almost goading me: "Go on, you know you want to. I've got so much more to give." At these speeds, traction is no longer an issue and the E-Class simply scampers forward at the first sign of provocation. There's a clear stretch ahead and I push on to 180mph, at which point the project takes on a whole new intensity.

The force curve is not linear, it's exponential. Roughly speaking, a car traveling at three times the national limit generates nine times the energy. At 200mph, any commercial airliner will already be airborne. "Both aerodynamically and mechanically, everything gets really serious when you top 200," says Gramm. "We learned a huge amount with the previous generation (205mph) EV12 and that helped us with this car." Creating a 220mph car is not easy – just ask Bugatti.

I spot a stream of trucks on the horizon and lift a little, passing them at little more than 170mph. It's a pointless exercise, of course. Hitting a truck at 200mph, 170mph or even 120mph would have the same calamitous effect, but at least it makes me feel better. God only knows what the trucker must have thought about being passed by a black missile at 4:45am. Maybe we woke him up.

My thoughts turn to the tires, which remain arguably the most critical component in any high speed run. The EV12 reached 350km/h while riding on Pirellis, but it's on Michelins today. "The Pirellis are rated for 350 and the Michelins for 340," explains Gramm. "But the Michelins – Pilot Sport Extra Loads – offer greater comfort." On this car they're filled with nitrogen so their pressure is less affected by temperature changes.

The road clears again and I can see for a mile ahead. I bury the throttle, but the acceleration is less urgent now. Every additional mph seems to be more of a struggle; it's almost as if we're going uphill. The needle swings past 300km/h, or 186mph. Brabus has had the speedo independently verified and we know at these speeds it's accurate to within a couple of km/h.

Hang on; be calm; don't make any sudden movements ... 310km/h. The wind and tire noise rises dramatically as the guard rail flashes past the window. It feels fast, f*cking fast. I try to straddle the center line, giving myself some room to maneuver. The road swings left and I apply a couple of degrees of steering lock. At 100mph you wouldn't even notice this curve, but at nearly 200mph it becomes a genuine challenge. The car feels light, even nervous, and I sense that so many of its parts are operating at or near their maximum capacity.

I'm feeling anxious and editor Bidrawn's words come back to me. "This silly little feature ain't worth the death of my favorite limey," he'd said. "And if you die, I'll haunt yer ghost till it's dead too." The road straightens out and I lean back on the gas ... 315km/h. Sorry Les, my ghost will have to wait.

318 ... 319 ... 320 (200mph) ... 321 ... I want to make sure ... 322 ... 323 ... The vibrations are huge and the wind rush extraordinary. On a public road, I'm traveling at a pace of which few cars have ever been capable, and I'm breaking no laws. From behind my right shoulder, photographer Salt calmly captures the moment, and then I hit the brakes.

Twelve- (yes twelve) piston front calipers crunch into 14.8 inch ceramic discs as the speedo needle sweeps left. This car stops even better than it goes. After what I've just experienced, 150mph feels pedestrian and I have to talk myself down to a more modest speed. The adrenaline is still pumping.

There will be those who will say that what I've just achieved is mad, foolhardy and downright irresponsible. Maybe they're right, but some things in life just need tobe done.

If Brabus is going to build a 200-plus-mph road car, then somebody will need to test it. And this morning, that somebody was me.

First printed in *European Car* magazine, December 2005

JAGUAR AT GOODWOOD

Driving a Jaguar C-type at the 2004 Goodwood Festival of Speed

Photographs IAN DAWSON

The Goodwood Festival of Speed began as a gathering of well-to-do enthusiasts back in 1993, but the hillclimb has since morphed into one of the most important dates in the motorsport calendar.

The idea was the brainchild of the Earl of March, owner of Goodwood House. While most British aristocrats faced with crippling death duties have turned their homes into museums, Lord March saw a business opportunity in Goodwood's motorsport heritage. The estate had housed a motor circuit between 1948 and 1966, when safety concerns forced its closure.

Lacking the requisite licence to reopen the circuit – that came in 1998 – the good Earl decided to host the event on his 1.16 mile-long driveway. Thirty thousand people turned up for the inaugural Festival of Speed and within a decade, Lord March was being forced to cap the attendance at 150,000, spread over three days.

In the early years, each run was timed and there was an element of competition. Nick Heidfeld set the official course record of 41.6sec (100.4mph) in 1999 at the wheel of a McLaren MP4/13 Formula One car. A fatal accident put an end to the serious competition in 2000, but most drivers still try hard.

There are famous race cars and 'bikes from every generation and many are reunited with their original drivers or riders. Sir Stirling Moss, John Surtees and Emerson Fittipaldi are regular attendees and, in 2006, even Nascar great Richard Petty took to the hill. There's a rally stage for famous rally cars and the parade of contemporary supercars has become increasingly popular.

I've been fortunate enough to drive up the hill on several occasions. My first experience of Goodwood was an attempt to steer a misbehaving Ford Mondeo Touring Car out of a busy paddock without running anyone over. Then I drove a 625bhp American Trans Am, whose keeper instructed me simply to "Drive it like you stole it." A drive in the supercar run in an Ascari KZ1 followed, but it was the drive in the Jaguar C-type that holds the fondest memories.

For all Jaguar's current woes – as I write Ford is trying to sell its problem child – there is something inherently charming about an old Jag. The C-type might have lacked the venomous power and muscularity of the D-type that followed, but it is still one of the most beautiful and desirable sports cars ever made. To drive it in front of so many people at such a famous event was a real privilege.

One of the other benefits of driving at Goodwood is that you sometimes get invited to the ball on the Saturday night. Hosted by Lord March in Goodwood House, it's attended by the great and the good of the motorsport world, all of whom enjoy dinner, a now-legendary firework display, and some big-name music.

There's an unwritten rule that what goes on inside stays inside, but suffice to say that superstar drivers are no better at drinking or dancing than the rest of us ...

NDU 289

Sitting in the paddock, trying to look like a racing driver (top left); leaving the startline, trying not to stall (top right)

Lord March's driveway looks awfully narrow when covered in water, framed by grandstands and viewed through the confines of a full face helmet. My right leg, jammed against the doorframe of a cockpit designed for someone half my size, begins to shake a little as I prod the C-type's throttle. The marshal, dressed in bright orange, calls me forward, eases me into position and then waves me on my way.

I have driven this C-type for a maximum of 400 yards and now I'm being asked to demonstrate its performance in front of 50,000 spectators at the Goodwood Festival of Speed. Jaguar only built 53 Cs and this is chassis number 45. It cost £2327 in 1953 and competed in that year's Mille Miglia. Today it's worth around £700,000 and it's not mine to crash.

The clutch bites and the rear-end does a merry jig as the age-old Dunlops fight for traction. Then we're away and up to second on the approach to the first 90° right-hander. I punch the brake pedal and guide the fluted nose towards the apex. It feels like walking pace but the car still steps out of line as I re-apply propulsive force. Then it straightens up again and I'm able to accelerate hard down the short straight in front of Goodwood House. I try not to think about the millions of TV viewers who will be watching my every move.

The C-type's 3.4-litre, 6-cylinder engine was pinched from the road going XK120, but subtle modifications increased its output to around 210bhp. In 1953 it became the first car to average more than 100mph at Le Mans and, in ideal conditions, it's capable of 0-60mph in 8.1sec and 144mph. Today, in the rain and on these tyres, it feels plenty quick enough. Sprinting past the main grandstand I see 6000rpm on the lovely Smith's instruments, before making the shift to third. I'm probably doing no more than 70-80mph but it feels much quicker. The rain is whacking my helmet and there's not enough airflow to remove it. My only option is to tweak open the visor and peak over the top of the tiny, non-original windscreen.

The tricky, blind left after the Molecomb grandstand requires a determined

punch on the middle pedal. Jaguar introduced disc brakes in the C-type for Le Mans in '53, but this production model makes do with drums. Their performance isn't as bad as many early racers, but they still represent a leap of faith for anybody stepping from a more modern machine. And the gearbox is terrible. Recalcitrant and unruly, it engages ratios with an ungentlemanly crunch. I hope the crowd can't hear.

Through the left-hander and up the slight rise of Pheasantry Hill before the famous flint wall looms alarming into view. We – the C-type and I – sweep right in front of it and then accelerate hard through the fastest part of the course to the finish. I'd like to think I top 100mph in third through this section. Then it's across the finish line and a gentle cruise to an assembly area at the top, in which we wait before returning to the paddock.

I clamber out and seek out the opinions of my fellow drivers. Although the C-type runs in Class 7, dedicated to European and American sports cars from 1950-65, we've been paired with a group of Indycars. Toyota's Cristiano Da Matta is standing beside the car in which he won the CART championship in 2002.

"We've got no tyre warmers," he explains. "There was absolutely no grip at all. I wanted to do a burn-out, but if I had, I'd still have been sat there. These cars require a different technique to Formula One. In an F1 car you brake all the way into the corner but in this, you tend to brake in a straight line before turning in. But it's been fun – it's like returning to an old friend." Sir Stirling Moss joins us, as does Christian Fittipaldi.

In such company, I feel like a fraud. I was in the toilet when God handed out driving talent and unlike certain other *Octane* contributors, I will never be described as a racing great. Instead, I've been parachuted into this foreign world to report on my experiences. As Rudyard Kipling might have put it; I am here to walk with Kings, while displaying the common touch.

After returning the C-type to the F1 paddock I make my way to the Dunhill Drivers' Club. There's only one entrance and it serves as a honeypot for autograph

hunters. Some are just enthusiastic children, but others are more sophisticated. Professional autograph hunters carry packets of photographs and bags of broken car parts. Earlier in the day, I'd witnessed Pedro de la Rosa being asked to sign a mangled piece of carbon fibre that once belonged to his F1 Jaguar.

The 'pros' offer me no more than a quizzical glance, but as I pause for photography, a young boy approaches and hands me a program. I try to explain that I'm just a journalist, but his Dad is already poised with a camera. So I scribble my name on his programme and hope that I haven't just wiped £100 off its EBay value. Then another arrives with a flag, and another with an autograph book. I feel silly, but at least it offers me an insight into what it must be like to be a genuine celebrity. There's no question that the attention is good for the ego but I wonder if the novelty would wear off.

Eventually there are no more trinkets to sign and I make my way inside the club. Billed as a private refuge for celebrity drivers, it offers catering facilities, a couple of display screens and a plethora of tables. Most of the time it resembles a motor racing Who's Who, but the atmosphere is relaxed and informal.

In the changing room, I meet Emerson Fittipaldi who is wearing what can only be described as tatty Y-fronts. This is not ideal – unless your hero is an attractive heroine, it is never good to meet them in their pants. "It is so wet out there," he muses, "and my car [a Penske Indycar from '94] is still geared for the Indy 500. I can't get out of first." Moments later 'Emmo', F1 World Champion in '72 and '74, slides into a set of Marlboro liveried overalls and order is restored. The Emperor has rediscovered his clothes.

It dries out over lunchtime, only to start raining again by the time I begin my second run. I'm feeling more confident now and there are less histrionics. At the top, it's raining more heavily, but this affords me the chance to talk to a solitary figure sitting, sheltered by an umbrella, in the Ferrari 312 T3 in which Gilles Villeneuve won the 1978 Canadian Grand Prix. The overalls are plain

Brazilian ex-F1 champion Emerson Fittipaldi with his clothes on; 'Emo' chews the fat with his nephew and ex-F1 driver Christian

and the helmet is bereft of sponsor's logos but its design and the eyes inside are instantly recognisable.

"This is the one and only time I'm going to drive it," says Jacques Villeneuve, who had flown in especially for the event. "It feels incredibly fragile. There's nothing here," he continues, grabbing the side panels. "I guess I'm used to driving safe racing cars." His thoughts are particularly poignant, given his father's tragic fate.

Scenes like this are central to the appeal of the Festival. Some drivers attend for contractual reasons, but many more turn up because it offers them a unique opportunity to catch up with old friends, both human and mechanical. In the same way, the spectators buy tickets because the Festival allows them to relive memories of yesteryear. The view from the driver's enclosure is undoubtedly different to that afforded by the grandstands, but the spirit is just the same.

And then there's the Goodwood Ball, hosted by the Earl of March on the Saturday night of the Festival. This is one of the social highlights of the motorsport year. Held at Goodwood House, it's attended by sponsors, drivers and other VIPs.

This year's entertainment was supposed to be provided by Brian Ferry but he pulled out at the last minute and was replaced by Blondie. Debbie Harry will be fifty next year but unless this is the (free-flowing) wine talking, she's still magnificent. There's an unwritten rule at such events that what goes on inside stays inside, but suffice to say that a good time was had by all and that superstar drivers are no better at drinking or dancing than the rest of us. The image of three hundred motoring luminaries rocking to '*Hanging on the telephone*' will stay with me for some time.

First printed in *Octane* magazine, September 2004

SMART IN BEIRUT

A tour of Beirut in a Smart Roadster-Coupé

Photographs STAN PAPIOR

In this age of 'car crash' TV, we rarely focus on the long term. The tsunami that devastated Southeast Asia on Boxing Day 2004, for example, grabbed the world's attention and filled front pages across the world. But, within weeks, if not days, the countries involved had begun rebuilding and the media had refocused its attention on David and Victoria Beckham. It was the same with the floods in New Orleans. Within days, the media world had become intoxicated by Victoria's new perfume and the Big Easy had been all but forgotten.

The same phenomenon affected Beirut. In the '80s and early '90s the Lebanese capital became infamous as the city in which western hostages were being held by the terrorist group, Islamic Jihad. Hitherto unknown names such as Brian Keenan, John McCarthy and Terry Waite suddenly entered public consciousness. Waite – the Archbishop of Canterbury's special envoy – spent four years in solitary confinement until he was released in 1991.

By then, the Civil War that had waged in Lebanon since 1975 had also finished and Beirut ceased to feature on the news agenda. With no disasters to report, this ancient city on the Mediterranean coast was left alone to rebuild. Beirut, the city until recently called 'the most dangerous in the world', could now enjoy a period of relative peace.

The city that I discovered a decade later couldn't have been more different to the traditional image of war-torn deprivation. This was a world full of supercars, Saudi royalty and vibrant nightlife. Late one afternoon, photographer Stan and I found ourselves chatting to a young Lebanese called Carla, an assistant in a Bang and Olufsen store.

"People in Lebanon like to show off their wealth," she explained. "Girls will spend their money on fashion, while guys buy cars and other toys. It's not unusual to find that people with a big car don't even own a house – they'll just live on a boat. That's also why we have so much valet parking in the city; everybody here wants to live like a king. Even the police ride Harley-Davidsons."

Was this hedonism the result of the war? "It was a war that nobody won and the new generations don't have the same feelings about it as the old. The Lebanese people are very ambitious; even during the war we were always rebuilding and we always had the latest brands."

Carla invited us to join her and some friends for a drink that night. We ended up at a rooftop bar, sipping Caipirinhas with some of the most forward-thinking young people you could ever hope to meet. Hard to believe that this was the Beirut of Waite and McCarthy.

Two years later, it was equally hard to believe that this new-found tranquillity should be shattered by an ugly war between Israel and Hezbollah, the paramilitary organisation based in Lebanon. The international airport into which we had flown was heavily bombed by Israeli forces and put out of action for two months. Such a shame.

M651311

The scars of war are still evident; anyone for bread?

It's almost 13 years since Terry Waite was driven from Beirut to Damascus and released by his captors, Islamic Jihad. Waite, envoy of the Archbishop of Canterbury, had been kidnapped in 1987 while trying to negotiate the release of western hostages in West Beirut. He spent the next 1763 days chained to a wall; over a thousand of them in solitary confinement.

Waite became a symbol of a land in turmoil. A civil war that erupted on 13 April 1975 between Palestinian exiles and Christian fundamentalists had, by the late '80s, dissolved into an anarchic free-for-all. By the time peace was restored in 1991, over 100,000 people had been killed and the city once dubbed 'the Paris of the East' lay in ruins.

Little has been heard of Beirut since those dark days, but the Lebanese capital has been undergoing a quiet renaissance. Money, both old and new, has flooded in, and an extensive rebuilding programme has been accompanied by a reawakening of the national psyche. Beirut is buzzing again, which is why, on a steamy Tuesday morning, I find myself driving a Smart Roadster-Coupé through the heart of the city.

My choice of transport might seem slightly absurd, but there is method in the madness. The launch of the brand in Lebanon at the beginning of June is a symbol of the city's changing ways, and a dealership in the suburbs is accompanied by a trendy glass showroom close to the city centre. If it really has become a Middle-Eastern haven for the style obsessed, then this self-conscious fashion car should be the perfect tool in which to explore it.

First impressions are frightening. The driving here is insane. Beirutis seem intent on testing the theory – espoused by a Dutch academic – that open, unregulated box junctions are safer because drivers concentrate harder. And they're all unregulated, because the traffic lights are largely ignored.

Driving here is a fraught business, and the feeling of insecurity is exacerbated by the diminutive roadster. Crossing three lanes of moving traffic with your head at bumper level is alarming and the problem's compounded by the irritatingly slow paddle-shift gearbox. A Hummer is what you need here: they're commonplace on these streets, looming at me from every angle like battleships over a rowing boat.

It's lunchtime and time to find a place to park. There are designated parking areas, but nobody seems to take too much notice. As a general rule, if you can find a place to plonk your motor that doesn't interfere with anyone else, then you're okay. It sounds like a recipe for anarchy, but works surprisingly well.

With the Smart resting, it's time to explore the pedestrianised central zone. This historical hub of Beirut used to lie on the so-called Green Line, the no-man's land between Muslim West and Christian East Beirut. For the best part of 16 years, this area was so deluged by bullets and mortars that no building was left unscathed. But to wander through it today is to witness an extraordinary transformation. Look closely and it's still possible to see the acned scars of gunfire, but the ambience is cool, chic and upmarket. Barricades have given way to cafés, where Gucci-clad young women strut about. It could be Paris or Milan.

The area around Nejmeh Square is home to government offices and armed guards patrol the street corners, but these 'bobbies on the beat' are reassuring rather than threatening.

It's now early evening and the rush-hour traffic is building steadily. From our vantage point on a roof-top café, it looks like a video game, with each car darting hither and thither in a search for road space. Students of chaos theory would love it.

We return to the Smart and take the long route back to the hotel. Beirut's coastline isn't as pretty as it might be but the sunset is still spectacular. This is the old West Beirut in which the Palestinian and Syrian forces once lived and died. Today, four- and five-star hotels sit side by side with shell-shocked buildings, some of which are earmarked for destruction. We pass the Hotel Riviera and its luxurious façade is no clue that it was here, 17 years ago, that Waite was taken hostage.

Next morning, we head to the east of the city for a meeting with Cesar Aoun,

'First impressions are frightening.
The driving here is insane.'

Smart's brand manager in Lebanon. I'm intrigued to find out who buys premium cars in this part of the world.

"We've sold 65 cars since we launched on 1st June," he explains. "Our customers are extroverted party people who are young at heart and want something different. The Roadster is proving harder to sell than the other cars because of the crazy driving. People need a big car in order to feel safe and a father wouldn't buy it for his son or daughter."

Midway through our meeting, Aoun's phone rings and there is a somewhat frantic exchange. 'That was a customer,' he says. 'He wanted his new car but I told him it wouldn't be ready until after lunch.'

This impatience is part of the Arab culture and to combat the problem, the dealership stocks over 50 new Mercedes and 35-40 Smarts. 'People buy on impulse and don't want to wait,' he says. 'If you had the cash, you could have a new Smart within an hour.' Everyone is also looking for a bargain. 'People walk in and say, "I will pay $15,000." I have to explain to them that I didn't grow it in my back garden.'

The Smart HQ is on the outskirts of town and it's interesting to note the contrast between the pristine ambience of the Beirut Central District (BCD) and these tired, noisy backstreets. To the south of the BCD, we stumble across a fascinating backstreet in a poor Muslim neighbourhood. The architecture is French colonial and these were once beautiful buildings, but today they are pockmarked with shell holes.

We return to the hotel to be greeted by the sight of a black Lamborghini Gallardo and a purple Murciélago. The former is registered in Kuwait while the latter bears the tell-tale graphics of Saudi Arabia. The scissor door opens on the Murciélago and a youth steps out to inspect the Smart. He can't be more than 18 years-old and his teeth carry the tracks of a sizeable brace.

'Very nice,' he mutters as I show him the cockpit. My new-found friend proceeds to explain that he's here for a three-week vacation and that he'd had the Lamborghini flown in specially. His name (Fahd) marks him out as a member of the Saudi Royal family and I nod approving towards his car – while wondering what it must be like to pilot such a motor around these mad, mad streets.

For a while I think that he must have the most outrageous car in Beirut, but this illusion is shattered a couple of hours later when I wander out of our restaurant to find a Mercedes-Benz SLR McLaren parked outside. It can be said without any exaggeration that supercar spotters are far better served in contemporary Beirut than they are in London or New York. Within a few miles I counted two Gallardos, a Ferrari 360 Modena, and numerous tuned Porsches, including a Techart GT2. Aoun even admitted to me that he'd sold a couple of Maybachs.

Towards the end of the trip, I've become better acclimatised to both the road conditions and my transport. The Roadster-Coupé is never going to deliver as pure a driving experience as a Mazda MX5, and with just 75bhp on offer, it's far from fast, but I'm still a fan. Some of the attention to detail is terrific and, importantly, it feels fun at low speeds. Wherever we go in Beirut our arrival is met with a smile and the locals are genuinely interested in this strange contraption. The Smart is a friendly sports car.

And Beirut is a friendly city. As Ferraris wrangle with Lamborghinis on the city streets, it is almost impossible to believe that, 15 years ago, this place was as much of a no-go area as Baghdad is today. That it has been able to rise from the ruins and reclaim so much of its former glory so quickly is a beacon of hope for all the world's troublespots. Be in no doubt: Beirut is back.

First printed in *Autocar* magazine, 5th October 2004

Beirut has no shortage of supercars – this is an Aston Martin Vanquish

MINI IN THE UNITED ARAB EMIRATES

Tackling the world's greatest drive

Photographs STAN PAPIOR

As a motoring journalist, there are two questions you're always asked at dinner parties: "What is the best car you've ever driven?" and "What is the best road in the world?" At the time of writing, the first is easy to answer. The Ferrari 599 is the best car I've ever driven. The second question, though, is much harder to call.

The world is full of great roads, and nearly all of them are easily accessible. Highway 1 in the US, which links San Francisco with Los Angeles, offers spectacular views but is compromised by too many slow moving tourists. The Col du Turini in France features '16 lacets' or hairpins and forms the most famous stage of the Monte Carlo Rally. One snowy day, I had a ride up the Col with rally legend Stig Blomqvist in an Audi S1 Group B rally car, which was an awesome experience.

There is a fantastic road than runs south from Tuscon, Arizona, to the border with Mexico. This is the heart of the old Wild West, where Cowboys fought Indians and men such as Wyatt Earp and Doc Holliday lived and died as legends. The road also passes the Davis Monthan Air force base, which plays home to some 3000 broken and retired aircraft. Billions of dollars worth of American military might sits idle and redundant just fifty miles north of the Mexican border.

For the more ambitious, there is a road through the Chobe National Park in Botswana. Best accessed from Zambia, Chobe is home to some 70,000 wild animals. Large concentrations of buffalo, hippo, giraffe and impala mix uneasily with predators such as lions, leopards and hyenas, but the park is most famous for its elephants. It's impossible to drive for long without seeing one of these magnificent creatures.

But there is another road in the United Arab Emirates, which arguably trumps them all. About an hour-and-a-half's drive from the building site that is Dubai, it climbs the Jebel Hafeet Mountain. In a country renowned for its excess, this road is opulence gone mad. Not only are the views spectacular, but so is the driving challenge.

What's nice about this road is its accessibility. Any tourist visiting Dubai can hire a car and experience its charms. And if you do decide to make the trip, be sure to visit the nearby camel market, which nestles on the border with Oman. I was offered my very own camel for £285 – tempting.

Credit for this story should also go to photographer Stan Papior. Stan has been Autocar *magazine's chief photographer since Moses was a boy, but he continues to produce some outstanding work. A version of this story also appeared on the US website,* Edmunds' Inside Line, *whose editors entered the pictures for a prestigious industry award. It was an award Stan won.*

The Jebel Hafeet Mountain Road can be found 90 minutes southeast of Dubai, next to the town of Al Ain and close to the United Arab Emirates' border with Oman. It's 7.3 miles long, comprises 60 corners and climbs nearly 4000ft from the plain below. And it is, without doubt, the greatest drive in the world.

Jebel Hafeet is an extraordinary place: the scene beyond the bonnet of our Mini convertible looks like it was rendered by a computer game designer after one Red Bull too many. Three lanes of immaculate highway – two up and one down – are carved into the limestone mountain in one, continuous squiggle.

Short, rapid straights are interspersed by sweeping curves that merge seamlessly from one to another. Some are to be taken at high speed with a single steering input and plenty of commitment; others are tight and technical, requiring patience and precision. There's more variation here than you'll find on the Col de Turini, or any of Europe's other classic roads.

The surface is also bereft of the potholes so popular with the Highways Agency. It feels like you could drive a Formula One car up here although, given our location, an A1 GP car might be more appropriate.

My charge today is less exotic. It seems hard to believe that BMW's first Mini rolled out of Oxford almost five years ago and that at the time, many believed that it would suffer the whims of fashion. By the end of 2005, however, Mini had sold 176,000 cars in the UK and the soft-top version is still the UK's best-selling convertible.

That the Mini has been such an astonishing success is due to much more than British patriotic fervour. While the Beetle is little more than a reskinned Golf, the Mini is arguably the best-engineered small car since the Issigonis original.

Its strength lies in its detailing. The Mini isn't cheap – the Cooper S we test here will set you back a cool £17,935 – but it feels like a quality product. The hood is taut and folds with the elegance and grace of Darren Gough on the dancefloor. Time and familiarity have also not dulled our enthusiasm for the cabin. Even the toggle switches, which at first seemed overwrought, retain their charm five years on. So what if the rear seats are all-but useless and the boot is only marginally bigger than the glovebox?

It is a few degrees cooler up the mountain than in Dubai, so we're able to run for long periods with the hood down (and the air-con off) and it's difficult not to be impressed. This is no blancmange of a car: BMW's engineers have managed to decapitate their baby without removing its soul.

'Jebel Hafeet is an extraordinary place: the scene beyond the bonnet looks like it was rendered by a computer game designer after one Red Bull too many.'
F دبي DUBAI 42037

The convertible isn't quite as sharp as the hatchback – that would be asking too much – but it's still fun. A Peugeot 206 CC or a Vauxhall Tigra would frustrate on this road, whereas the Mini warms to the task. Body flex is minimal, the steering positive and the Cooper S's 170 horses are just enough to cope with the gradient. The harder I push, the more it responds and the more pleasure it offers.

If the Mini's engineers deserve honouring for their services to small-car design, then the engineer responsible for the Jebel Hafeet Mountain Road should receive a knighthood. The variety of bends is so great that it must have been designed by an enthusiast, but its origins are shrouded in mystery.

You can buy an enormous guidebook detailing the hydrogeology of the local spring or the DNA of the resident butterflies, but the history of a road that must have cost £50m to build proves almost impossible to trace. Desperate for more information, I seek out the manager of the Mercure hotel at the top of the mountain. Rajesh Kapoor reckons that it "was completed about a dozen years ago. I think the designer was Swedish because we had a Swedish guest to stay who claimed that her husband was responsible for it." But that contradicts a claim made in a natural history guidebook that the road was built in 1987.

Official sources suggest it was built as a honey pot for tourists who travel from nearby Dubai or Abu Dhabi to sample the mountain air. But with the exception of the mediocre hotel, there's almost nothing here. The road culminates in a gargantuan paved car park, but the tatty café and Portaloo would not look out of place in Weston-super-Mare.

Perhaps the real, unspoken reason for the road's existence is to be found a couple of kilometres from the hotel. There, sitting atop the mountain is a huge palace belonging to Sheikh Zayed bin Sultan Al Nahyan, ruler of the Emirates until his death in 2004. His face also adorns a huge banner at the entrance to the road and it's under his watch that it was constructed. It is incredible to think that this extraordinary feat of engineering is, in reality, little more than a private driveway. It's enough to make Goodwood owner Lord March green with envy.

Late in the evening, photographer Papior and I return to the Sheikh's old driveway. From a vantage point about halfway up the mountain, we're able to look down on a dramatic twist of Tarmac that is now bathed in neon. The streetlamps, of which there must be 500, are tuned to light not only the road, but also the adjacent rock. At Le Mans, 230mph racecars must light the Mulsanne for themselves; here in the Emirates, an empty road is slow-roasted by half a million watts.

... look down on a dramatic twist of Tarmac that is now bathed in neon.

In search of a new pet – the market on the border with Oman offers 1500 camels for sale, priced from £285

Further down the mountain we find a series of lurid tyre marks, suggesting that we're not the only enthusiasts taking advantage of this motoring nirvana. Black paint on one of the border posts even suggests that some might have been trying a little too hard. Our friendly hotelier reckons that Land Rover's test engineers have used the mountain for hot-weather testing and that Porsche's employees will soon be paying a visit.

Today is Saturday, but the traffic is still laughably light. And because there are two lanes all the way up the mountain, stray vehicles can be picked off quickly and easily. The benefits of this cannot be underestimated. The most sensational Alpine pass can turn you purple with frustration if you end up trapped behind a truck, and even at the Nürburgring Nordschleife you can be harassed by bikers or camper vans. Here on the mountain there are no such worries.

Swapping between second, third and occasionally fourth gear makes good use of the 162lb-ft of torque. The new Mini's engine will be turbocharged, but I will miss the whine and shove of this car's supercharger.

It's fascinating to watch the reaction of the locals to our orange wonder. The Mini might be ubiquitous in the UK, but in this part of the world it's still a novelty. In Dubai, the BMW 7-series outsells the 5-series which outsells the 3-series, and only a few hundred Minis are bought each year in the whole of the Middle East. No wonder the sight of two westerners in a tiny convertible is the cause of much hilarity.

Late in the morning I indulge myself with a final blast up the hill. It takes around eight-and-a-half minutes to complete all 60 corners and scale the UAE's highest mountain. And while I'm sure I would have had more outright enjoyment in something with twice the power and rear-wheel-drive, there are few cars in the Mini's price bracket that can entertain like this on this kind of road.

And what a road. As a means of servicing a palace, it must stand as one of the most extravagant, self-indulgent and fantastic enterprises ever undertaken. It really is the world's greatest drive, in every sense.

First printed in *Autocar* magazine, 24th January 2006

'If the Mini's engineers deserve honouring for their services to small-car design, then the engineer responsible for the Jebel Hafeet Mountain Road should receive a knighthood.'

1988 LINCOLN TOWN CAR

BABE RALLY

Driving a $177 car from the Big Apple (BA) to the Big Easy (BE)

Photographs TOM SALT

I've always thought that the British have an ill-informed view of the United States. If Brits go on holiday, we tend to go to New York, Orlando or the west coast cities of Los Angeles and San Francisco. All are relatively liberal, cosmopolitan and, in the case of New York, not too dissimilar to London.

Comparatively few of us ever bother to stop in the so-called 'flyover states' and, in particular, the Deep South. Those who have never visited the deeply religious, gun-toting Republican heartlands tend to underestimate just how conservative huge swathes of the US really are – for good or bad.

If you'd only read the leftist British media, you could be forgiven for thinking that John Kerry was a shoe-in for the 2004 election. My first inkling that this wouldn't be the case came some months earlier on a domestic flight from Phoenix to Tucson, Arizona. Some mention was made of Kerry and the elderly guy sat next to me hissed that he was "too liberal". Others soon joined in the commotion and I quickly realised that Kerry was doomed. By December, Bush was back in power on a landslide.

This is part of the reason why I find the US so fascinating. While the anti-globalisation protestors criticise the massive reach and common culture of McDonald's and Coca Cola, the US itself remains an extraordinarily diverse and, indeed, divided country. It is home to some of the most bizarre and interesting characters you are ever likely to meet, and half of them seemed to be taking part in the BABE Rally.

The idea of driving from the Big Apple (New York) to the Big Easy (New Orleans) in a car that had cost no more than $250 really captured my imagination. Here was a chance to leave behind the exotica and indulge in a 'real' motoring adventure with some like-minded folk.

At first, I didn't fancy my chances of finding any sort of car for the cash, let alone one that could transport me 1500 miles across the American South. It was only thanks to the support and generosity of my fellow competitor, Tim Hansen, that this story became possible. Without him, we'd never have found our Lincoln Town Car which, as far as I know, he's still using to this day.

In my opinion, too many people believe that enjoying motoring means spending lots of money on flashy equipment. I don't, for example, enjoy the forced bravado that too often accompanies European track days. The BABE Rally was proof that you can have a good time on the road, whatever your budget.

The rally was tremendous fun, but it was not without its moments of sadness. I'll never forget arriving in New Orleans to witness the devastation caused by Hurricane Katrina. The Big Easy no longer featured on the media agenda, and I had foolishly imagined that the richest country in the world would have quickly rebuilt one of its most famous cities.

As soon as we crossed into the city it became clear this was not the case. Driving through deserted streets and talking to the handful of people trying to resurrect their homes, was a deeply moving experience. It was hard to believe that I was still in the so-called United States of America.

FRANK SR.
BABE
10
baberally.com

The Trashwagon (left) – a very sorry Subaru; Miles Fox is one of life's characters

BABE stands for Big Apple to Big Easy. It's a simple challenge – drive from New York to New Orleans in a car you've purchased for less than the humble sum of $250. Along the way, you will be asked to compete in numerous challenges and the most successful team will be the winner of a worthless prize.

It is a challenge beautiful in its simplicity, but tricky in its logistics. The US is a huge place and Manhattan isn't brimming with $250 junkers. The chances of us turning up in New York on the day of the rally and buying a car were just about nil.

A cry for help was issued through the rally's online forum and another competitor, Tim Hansen, answered our call. Hansen is just 26 but has bought and sold more than 60 cheap cars. He suggested something Japanese but that wasn't in keeping with an American adventure. For us, there was only one choice: a giant lump of Detroit iron.

At 10:30pm one Friday night, I received an email from Hansen claiming that he'd found the perfect tool – a 1988 Lincoln Town Car, which was being offered on eBay. Half an hour later and after a frantic bidding war, we'd secured our place on the grid. A classic piece of eighties Americana was ours for the paltry sum of $177. JR Ewing would've been proud.

Fast forward two months and you find us on Staten Island, New York, inspecting the competition. Twenty-five teams have gathered for the get-to-know-you dinner, and there's an eccentric array of metal. A tatty looking MG Midget sits apologetically beside a huge van of the type popularised by BA Baracus, and a Yugo Zastava, which has been smeared in creosote and fitted with twin, side-mounted exhausts.

We're beginning to think we might have underestimated this challenge. While all the teams have bought their cars cheaply, most have been several months in preparation. Even now, an army of tools is being employed as last minute checks are made.

This is a worry. Team Top Gear's mechanical knowledge amounts to a GCSE in Design Technology. Our 'back-up' consists of a roll of masking tape, a tyre pressure gauge and a can of engine oil, bought from the local Walmart.

At around 11pm, our Town Car rumbles into view. One of the other competitors, Louis Tennant, had kindly agreed to deliver it for us. "It's running fine," he says. "There's only half an exhaust but that just makes it sound like a Nascar." We hurriedly shut the door and kiss it goodnight. So far so good.

Our optimism is short-lived. On the short drive from the hotel to the start-line, an oil warning light flickers into life. We prise open the bonnet and lob in a quart of oil. "You're using 5W oil are you?" says a rival. "I wouldn't have risked that.

Cruising in a Lincoln – J R Ewing would have been proud; flying the English flag outside the Capitol, Washington DC

It's the wrong viscosity." Team TG has already been revealed as a bunch of British idiots and we haven't even left the start-line.

A chubby figure in a red boiler suit wanders over. His hairstyle is pinched from the 1960s and his round spectacles boast a natty pair of clip-ons. "Tim Hansen," he says, "glad the car made it." Hansen's eccentricities are well cultivated and he's become the subject of a fly-on-the-wall documentary. For the next few days he'll be followed by a cameraman who refuses to mix with the crowd for fear of compromising his artistic integrity. This event gets stranger by the minute.

Today's route takes us south-west past Philadelphia and Washington to Harrisonburg, a nondescript town in Virginia. We're being advised to stick to the highway, but I've never been to the White House, so we make a detour. George W's gaff is surrounded by security fencing and agitated officials.
"Toenee Blair is coming," says a helpful tour guide, "he's kinda like the president of the United Kingdom."

Day one is also providing the first taste of the BABE Rally competitions. Each day we're to be given a challenge to complete and today's involves playing car snooker. A digital photograph of a red car must be followed by an appropriate colour, with pink scoring highest. Hapless punters are being pursued and snapped by a bunch of eccentrics in crap cars.

These endeavours are not without incident. We arrive in Harrisonburg to learn that the driver of a Honda CRX-based three-wheeler is in trouble with the law. A driver took offence to having his photograph taken and called the police. Now, the officer is trying to determine whether the tricycle is legal. Determined to assert his authority, he eventually hands over a ticket for a cracked windscreen.

The incident highlights a peculiarity of the US system. "There's no vehicle testing procedure in Michigan," says John Deikis, the Honda's owner. "As long as you have the title documents and a VIN number you can register the car."

He bought the CRX for a dollar after it was involved in an accident. "We welded together a tubular rear-end and used it to go ice racing for a couple of years, before we registered it for this event." The personalised number plate, which reads (BA2BE) cost $38 and is the car's most expensive feature.

Deikis travelled 670 miles just to reach the start-line, but his commute was not the longest. Tommy Gallagher and Patrick Weise drove 3000 miles from San Diego, only for their '88 Oldsmobile to shear a control rod within 100 miles of the start. It took most of day one to fix it, but they're still in the rally.

Day two continues the journey southwest to the state of Tennessee. Over breakfast, Hansen is looking worried. "Miles Fox and the Trashwagon have

Sequoyah
CAVERNS

'We're a pathetic sight, but after a thousand miles of competition,
I've grown quite fond of the giant, rusting turd.'

Disaster! The power steering is no more (left); cruising Bourbon Street at the end of the rally (right)

blown a head gasket," he says, "we're going to help them." A convoy of six cars leaves in pursuit of the mysterious Fox.

An hour later, we discover a sorry looking Subaru and an even sorrier looking youth. Dressed in a leather flying bonnet and combat trousers, the unkempt Fox is trying to rescue his beloved 'Trashwagon' with a pot of engine sealant. After an hour's hard labour, the Subaru is reborn. Only two cylinders are functioning, but he'll give it a go.

We prepare to leave, only to be met by a disaster of our own. The Town Car appears to be urinating on the car park. A cluster of worried faces peer underneath and their diagnosis is simple: the power steering pump has given up on life. For the next 1000 miles, I'm going to have to muscle this 2.5-tonne car and hope that the steering column hangs together. Could be worse, I guess. At least we're still mobile.

We arrive in Newport minus the Trashwagon, which has now coughed its final splutter. The rest of the party is in fine form, although some are clearly taking the competition more seriously than others. "It's the same with any rally," says the event organiser, Justin Clements. "Some people take it incredibly seriously, while most are just happy to get to the finish."

Clements also runs the ever-popular Staples2Naples rally in Europe, but this is the first time he's organised an event here in the United States. "The biggest problem is the size of the place," he says, "it's a logistical nightmare." Day 3 is the biggy. The route cuts across country through the tourist trap of Gatlinburg and on to the infamous Tail of the Dragon at Deals Gap, an 11-mile twist of tarmac boasting 318 corners. We're entering the Deep South; the land made famous by Jack Daniels, the civil rights movement and Daisy Duke.

Gatlinburg boasts its own tribute to The Dukes of Hazzard in a recreation of Cooter's Garage. Inside, hanging from a wooden beam are four pairs of denim shorts cut too high and too small. It's like coming face to face with the Holy Grail.

An hour later, we arrive at the Deals Gap, which boasts corners called 'Pearly Gate', 'Hog Pen Bend' and 'Crud Corner'. The scene outside the café is reminiscent of the Nürburgring Nordschleife on a public day. Except that most of the bikers are on Harleys, not Fireblades, and they're wearing wife-beater vests instead of 'sporty' garish leathers.

The Town Car was never built for such roads and the absence of power steering makes it doubly challenging. We crawl our way across the mountainside at little more than walking pace. We're a pathetic sight, but after a thousand miles of competition, I've grown quite fond of the giant, rusting turd.

Twenty years ago, the Town Car was the preferred choice of America's golfing class and it's packed with electric gizmos, most of which still work. Touch the door

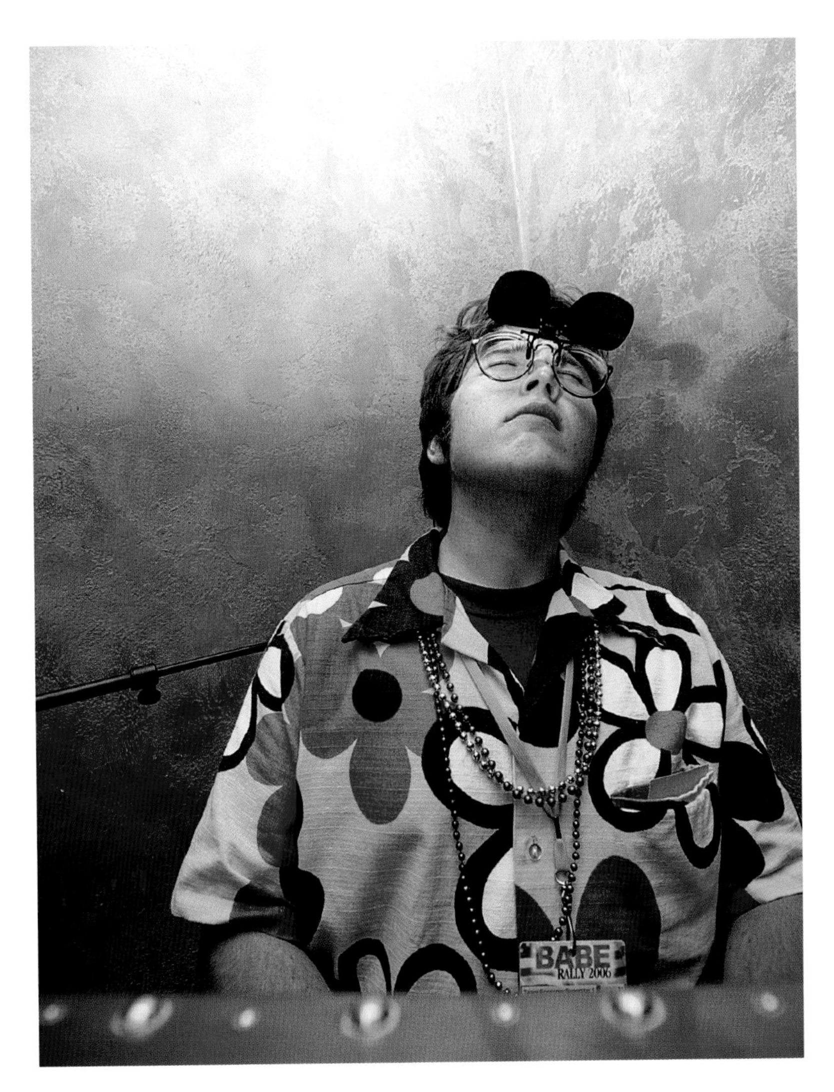

The impact of Hurricane Katrina is still all-too evident; Tim Hansen (right) in a familiar pose

handle and the lock illuminates, the trunk lid shuts by itself and a tiny joystick controls the electric seats. There's even a thermometer attached to the driver's wing mirror, which is illuminated at night.

Only the seats cause concern. The air-conditioning packed in long ago and the plasticky leather trim has been marinated in God knows how much sweat. It's a horrible thought and, having discovered that the last owner was a male college student, we've declared the back seat a no-go zone.

We stop for the night in Fort Payne, Alabama, where it seems you can't drink beer in a hotel car park. Our attempt to do so is met by an official complaint and a visit from a state trooper. "If you don't take that inside you'll be coming to the station with me," says the menacing man with the big gun. "This state has only been wet [allowed alcohol] for six months and people are still getting used to it. We don't have bars and we don't have hootchy-cootchy [strip] clubs in Alabama."

We're soon back on the highway and heading straight for New Orleans. We settle back with the cruise control set to 70mph, marvelling at the brilliance of our $177 car. Even when the rest of the exhaust falls off with a hundred miles to go, our enthusiasm is unabated. It just makes the five-litre V8 sound even better. This car is like Mick Jagger – its best days are behind it, but it can still work some magic.

Our arrival in New Orleans conjures mixed emotion. There is no mistaking the impact of Hurricane Katrina: a boat lies stranded by the central reservation; the word 'help' is scrawled on a rooftop. In the suburbs, people are living in mobile homes as they rebuild their lives. "I finished renovating this house three days before the storm," says a bemused local. "Now I must start again." He reckons less than a third of the population will return.

Other parts of the city are doing their best to carry on as normal. The famous French Quarter was largely unaffectedby the storm and its hedonism contrasts sharply with our experiences of the Bible Belt. Beautiful architecture is offset by garish bars and strip joints ... 'Hustler Barely Legal' anyone?

The rally ends with another New Orleans tradition. At the prize-giving party we stand on a balcony and lob beaded necklaces at the girls below in the hope – often fulfilled – that they'll reveal their boobs. It's a bizarre finale to a bizarre event.

BABE doesn't have the supercars and razzmatazz of the Gumball Rally, but it's much more honest. Wealthy professionals mixed easily with hard-up students; only one car failed to make the finish and everyone had a good time. The BABE Rally is motoring in the raw, and all the better for it.

First printed in *Top Gear* magazine, October 2006

FERRARI ACROSS CHILE & BOLIVIA

A drive through Chile and Bolivia in a Ferrari 599

Photographs TOM SALT

Travel to any backpacker destination in the 'third world' and you'll be offered T-shirts bearing the image of Che Guevara. It always amuses me that the Argentinian-born Marxist revolutionary should have become such a friend of the capitalist street trader, keen to make a quick buck. It's intriguing to wonder how much either the street sellers, or those who proudly wear the T-shirts, really know about the guerrilla warrior who was executed in Bolivia in 1967.

I wonder, too, what El Che would have made of me becoming the first person to drive a Ferrari through Bolivia. Surely such a symbol of capitalistic excess would have offended his sensibilities? Or would he have harnessed the power of Ferrari's 620 horses to revolutionary effect?

My escapade through northern Chile and into Bolivia formed a leg of the Ferrari Panamerican 20,000. Similar in concept to the 15,000 Red Miles trip across China, (see page 8), the Panamerican tour saw two Ferrari 599s complete a 20,000 mile tour of south, central and north America. As before, I had requested a challenging leg and, once again, I was not disappointed. We were crossing lands unknown to the guide book and staying in places beyond the reach of even the most ambitious backpacker.

Critics of these expeditions point to the size of the Ferrari entourage, which, on this occasion, stretched to eighteen people. We travelled most of the time in convoy and at a modest pace. At times this proved frustrating, but I could understand the logic. The leader of the trip, Enrico Goldoni, had staked his reputation on getting two £200k cars through some of the most challenging and dangerous countries on earth. It's no surprise that he wanted to keep them close to his chest.

On the one occasion when I left the convoy, photographer Tom Salt and I were given a taste of our vulnerability. Having stopped for a photograph, we lost sight of the other vehicles. We also lost radio communication, there was no cell phone reception, we were at least fifty miles from the nearest settlement, and I was in a Ferrari with limited fuel and no spare tyre. It was one of those moments when you think, 'What happens next?'

Other cynics argue that the tours are insensitive. In China, I had witnessed an old man pulling the feathers off a bird in the gutter, and there were similar displays of poverty in Bolivia. In such circumstances, is it right to blow by in such an opulent car?

In China, Ferrari's PR guru, Antonio Ghini had justified it in these terms. "Italy was poor in the post-war period, but a Ferrari was a stimulating message, an inspiration. I believe it can play the same role in China today." The same argument applied in South America, and it as an argument with which I agree. The reaction of the locals to our arrival was invariably positive, and there can be no denying that our travelling circus brought useful income to these communities.

For those who took part, this was a great adventure, I hope this is reflected in the story.

The two Australian tourists look a little bemused. They've spent two days travelling from the glamour of Sydney to the tiny tourist trap of San Pedro de Atacama only to be confronted by that most potent symbol of first world opulence, the Ferrari. Blocking the narrow, dusty street are two 599 GTB Fiorano's and they're surrounded by a red-shirted crew, speaking quick-fire Italian and towing personalised luggage.

Café owners and tour guides, anxious to share in the kafuffle, reach for their camera phones, while mangy looking dogs scan the area for scraps of food. The Australians grab a happy snap, wish us good luck and leave this extraordinary scene. Welcome to northern Chile and the bizarre world of the Ferrari Panamerican 20,000.

For the next five days, I shall be joining this 20,000 mile adventure, which began at a Fiat factory in Belo Horizonte, Brazil on August 24th and is due to end in New York on November 17th. The Ferrari caravan arrived from Argentina last night and today we'll start the journey north, before we tack west into Bolivia, reaching the city of La Paz by Friday. It's a distance of around a thousand miles and every one should be an experience.

"The next few days will be one of the toughest legs of the tour," says Enrico Goldoni, as he hands me a radio and ushers me into the blue 599. In normal life, Goldoni has the enviable job of orchestrating Ferrari's roadtest team, but now he must lead two supercars across some of the world's most dangerous countries. "It was difficult leaving Maranello [Ferrari HQ] but getting the cars through such varied terrain is a huge challenge. This is really a crazy thing to do." Goldoni leads a support crew of eighteen people, who travel in a mix of Iveco vans and tiny Fiats.

We leave en masse and trundle through dusty streets, past modest buildings that have a ramshackle quality some might call 'character'. Situated in the picturesque heart of northern Chile, San Pedro de Atacama is a relatively comfortable haven for ambitious tourists who've made the journey north from the capital, Santiago, west from Argentina, or south from Peru. Most will soon move out again, crammed into age-old buses or 4x4s.

My transport is less modest. In the UK, a 599 retails for £177,325, but by the time you've plucked a few choice items from the options list – Scuderia Ferrari shields are a snip at £1045 – the price can easily spiral towards £200k. The Panamerican cars have been modified for the trip, but only slightly. The ground clearance has been raised by 25mm and the underbody wears protective aluminium cladding to cope with the tricky terrain. For this leg of the journey, the car also boasts specially developed Pirelli rally-spec tyres, which offer increased traction in the sand and dust.

Today's stage is relatively short and so we indulge ourselves with a visit to the Valle La Luna. An eon of floods and wind has created a scene that, as its name suggests, resembles the surface of the moon. It would be surreal enough without the presence of two Ferraris and if you were a conspiracy theorist, you really could imagine Neil Armstrong taking "one small step for man" in the dusty desert.

Eventually, we drag ourselves away and head north to the copper mining town of Calama. We travel everywhere in convoy, with Goldoni leading the way in a Fiat Idea. At times it's frustrating, but it's also sensible. Even the good roads in Chile can be strewn with rocks and the occasional Llama.

I drove a Ferrari 612 Scaglietti across western China last year, but this is my first experience of its smaller, more sporting sibling. The 599 is billed as a front-engined, V12 Ferrari of the old school. Its lineage is derived from the 365 Daytona, but this is a thoroughly modern machine. Whereas the Daytona's 4.4-litre V12 mustered 352bhp, the Fiorano's 6.0 V12 produces 620bhp.

It is incredible to think that this everyday production Ferrari is faster than the F40 supercar of 1989. "The tyre technology was nowhere near as good back then," says Goldoni. "The F40 was a challenging car to drive hard." He should know – Goldoni was the man responsible for the F40's brakes and suspension.

Taking a break on the Atacama Salt Flats in northern Chile; the 599 is automotive art

Contrasting emotions on the Bolivian border; power sliding on the Salar De Uyuni – naughty

We go to bed early in Calama, in anticipation of a long day ahead. We're to drive 393km (244miles) across the Bolivian border to the town of Uyuni and it's not long before the paved highways give place to dirt roads. At speeds of just 30-40mph we plod on, guzzling the dust of the car in front. We're at an altitude of 4000m (over 13,000ft) and both the 599 and I are struggling for breath. A surgeon – hired for the occasion – monitors my progress, while the mechanics keep a wary eye on the car.

The rolling landscape, interspersed with the occasional lake or salt flat, is remarkable. So many of the problems that irritate me in 'real life' – voicemail, dishonesty, Ken Livingstone – seem irrelevant here. There can be no denying that travel is good for the mind.

The experience is made doubly surreal by my choice of transport. The luxurious ambience inside the leather-lined cabin seems to bear no relation to the view beyond the bonnet. I've been in IMAX cinemas that felt more real.

For two hours we drive without seeing anybody else, and then we arrive at a Police checkpoint at Ascotan. At least a hundred miles from any notable civilisation, it's occupied by a solitary official, a dog and an old railway carriage. The facilities are basic and the climate can be cruel – a giant icicle dangles precariously from a water tap. Our host seems under-whelmed by our entourage as he checks our paperwork, raises the gate and ushers us on our way. Two hours later, I'm at the wheel of the first Ferrari ever to enter Bolivia.

In contrast to Chile, which has recovered well since General Pinochet left office in '89, Bolivia is still brutally poor. "We have all the resources of a rich country but we've been let down by poor administration," says our guide, Dante. This is not Africa – the people are not starving – but the country is under-achieving. The incumbent President, Evo Morales, is openly courting Castro, which has not pleased the entrepreneurial classes.

It's already dark by the time we reach Uyuni and we've been driving for over fourteen hours. A hasty dinner is followed by a night of deep sleep. In the morning I awake to discover dusty streets filled with elderly, dilapidated people. Three dogs are contriving to have sex on the pavement, finding some hedonistic escape. The poverty is self-evident and it's quite a culture shock after the relative affluence of Chile.

In such an environment, the Ferraris look incongruous and some will argue that it's wrong to bring such a potent symbol of western affluence to such a place. I do not subscribe to that view – we're fuelling the local economy and Ferraris, even in the developed world, have always been slightly otherworldly.

Uyuni's modest tourist trade is supported by the extraordinary Salar De Uyuni. Measuring over 10,000 square kilometres, it's the world's largest salt flat and an incredible sight. We spend a couple of happy hours driving the 599 on the salt and visiting the bizarre Playa Blanca hotel. Boasting just a handful of rooms, the hotel is constructed entirely of salt. Would you like chips with that sir?

It's late afternoon by the time we leave Uyuni, which proves to be a mistake. The journey to Potosí is little more than 200km but it takes us nine hours. On rutted dirt roads, we crawl along at 15mph with the 599's steering wheel shaking violently in my sweaty palms. The closest most Ferrari owners will come to such terrain is a kerb hop in Chelsea.

Out of the dust and gloom, I can just make out the mix of vertical cliff faces and sheer drops that line the road. From time to time we creep through tiny communities, their residents no doubt bemused to witness the sight of two supercars kicking up dust. One wonders whether they really know what they're seeing.

As we near Potosí, we're also forced to dice with overenthusiastic minibuses and taxi drivers, who have little interest in self-preservation. At a little after midnight, a twenty-year old Mercedes minibus cuts across my bows and misses me by inches. It's a relief when, at 1am, we arrive safely at our hotel.

Potosí is the world's highest city at 4090m and in the 18th century, silver

'The V12 has the most erotic soundtrack. Time and again I find myself shifting down, just to hear it crescendo once more.'

mining made it the richest in Latin America. It's declined since but much of its architecture retains a baroque beauty. The central square could have been plucked from Prague or Budapest and it's packed with a vibrant mass of humanity. Their spirit is in denial of the altitude – while I pant and wheeze, they scurry busily on their way. It would have been nice to spend more time here, but we must push on to La Paz.

The road to Bolivia's commercial capital is quick and paved, to the relief of us all. The cars and their occupants have been taking a battering and the journey across the Altiplano has not been entirely trouble free.

A damaged wire has obliterated the dashboard electronics on my car and a tyre was ripped near the Chilean border. The latter was fixed immediately and the dashboard will be repaired during tomorrow's rest day. Ferrari is carrying a van full of parts and should the worst happen, there's a spare car waiting in Italy.

There can be no denying that the Ferraris have handled the terrain remarkably well. Gone are the days when the products of Maranello were no more than a weekend play thing, to be cherished and protected. The 599 is comfortable and practical enough to be used as an everyday tool, which has to be a good thing. If you owned this Ferrari, you'd want to use it.

On the final run to La Paz, the road opens up and I'm at last able to exploit its potential. In perfect conditions, this car will hit 60mph from rest in just 3.9sec and reach 205mph. The altitude in Bolivia has slaughtered some of the horses, but it's still on the quick side of rapid and with 448lb ft of torque available, it's extremely flexible.

The V12 also has the most erotic soundtrack. Quiet enough at cruising speeds never to become tiresome, it responds to a determined prod of the throttle with a soulful howl. Time and again I find myself shifting down, just to hear it crescendo once more. Premiership footballers might lean towards the V8-engined F430, but a V12 Ferrari remains the purist's choice.

The paddle-shift gearchange is also the best I've experienced. Even a generation ago, these systems were disappointingly crude, but the software has now been developed to the point where I'd choose it over the manual alternative. It seems to fit the 599's comfortable yet engaging character. This Ferrari is undeniably expensive but it's difficult to think of a rival that offers such a potent mix of virtues. Anyone who lusted after a Daytona as a child would be well served by the 599 today.

We arrive in La Paz in the early evening to be met by that potent symbol of civilisation, the Burger King. After so many days on the road, it feels odd to be back in a jostling metropolis. The Ferrari caravan will rest here tomorrow and after a reception at the Italian embassy, they'll roll on to Peru.

I'm disappointed not to be joining them. The last few days have been fascinating for the things I've seen and the people I've met. Ferrari's Panamerican 20,000 is a PR stunt but that doesn't invalidate the challenge. Some of the places we've seen have a natural beauty to match anything on earth, but they don't feature in guide books and they're inaccessible to conventional tourists. My new-found Australian friends don't know what they missed.

First printed in *Octane* magazine, January 2007

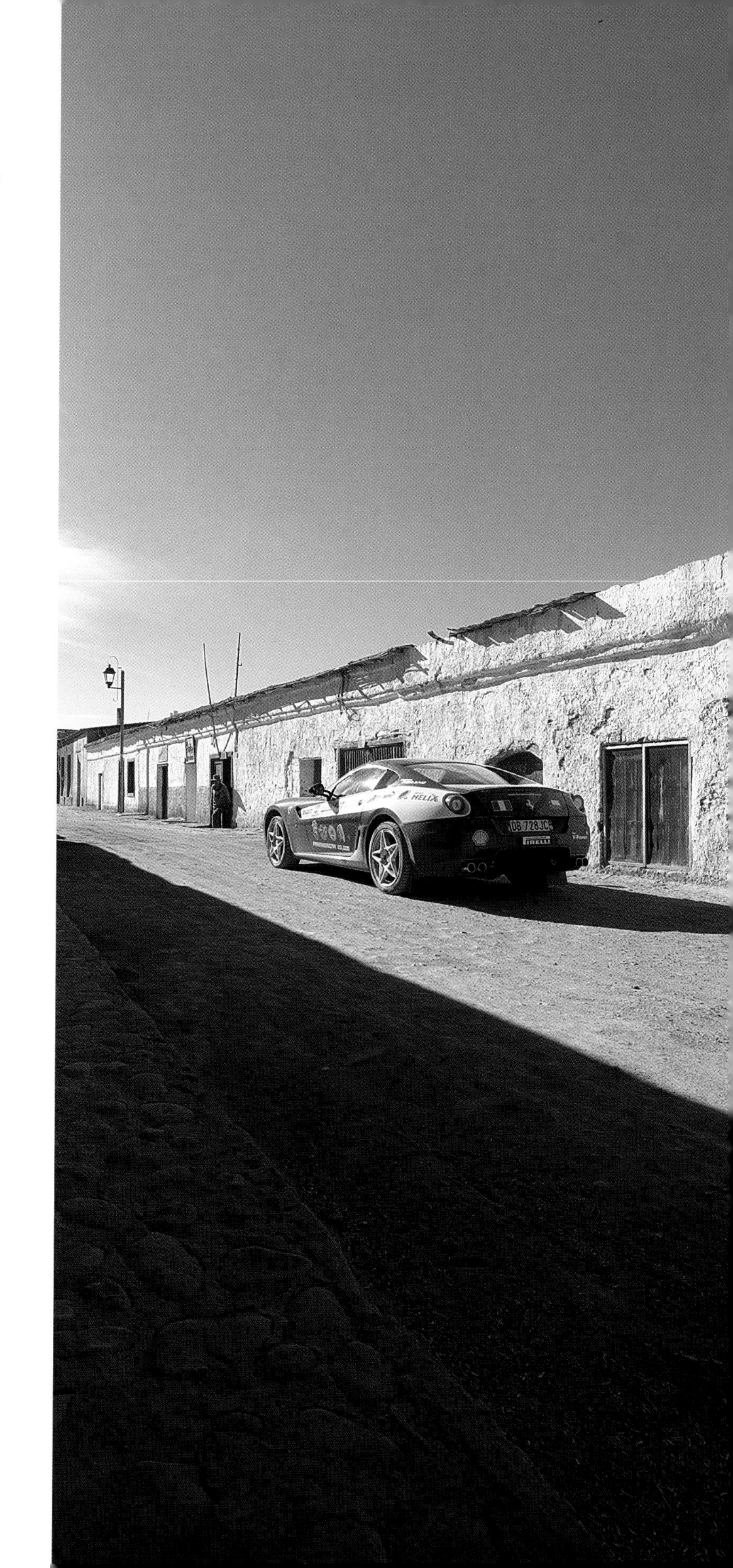

Bolivian locals are bemused by the arrival of two Ferraris; visibility is a problem on the dirt roads

LAND ROVER IN RIO

Touring Rio de Janeiro in a Discovery

Photographs ANTON WATTS

When I travel, I'm always accompanied by a photographer, and often, by a local guide. Many of the adventures I've had over the past few years would have been impossible without the presence of someone who speaks the local language and who knows of a world beyond the Lonely Planet *guidebook. Sometimes, they also serve as a security guard – without a black guide in Soweto, for example, I'd have been a vulnerable target.*

The quality of the guides can vary dramatically, though, and you never know what you're going to get. The best are a source of enlightenment, taking you to unusual places and introducing you to fascinating characters. Without a guide in Sao Paulo (see p162) we would never have met Maria Jose Clemente, and the story would have been infinitely poorer. In Soweto our guide, Thami, became an intrinsic part of the story. Young, intelligent and aspirational, he was not about to waste the opportunity presented by black empowerment.

But the worst guides can suck the energy out of a trip. I once travelled around South Korea with a guide who made a strange whining noise, rather like a chainsaw, at the first hint of a stressful situation. In unfamiliar towns, she would also insist on being taken to the local police station to ask for assistance. Nor did it help that she developed a crush on photographer Tom Salt, or 'Mr Salt' as she called him. On day two this was an irritation, but by day 10, I was ready to dump her by the roadside.

Our guide in Rio, Sylvanha, was somewhere in between. She was a local student and sometime TV production assistant who was earning extra money taking business people around her home town. In a country famous for its inequality, Sylvanha belonged to the privileged few and toured everywhere in her new car. She was 25, affluent and surprisingly enlightened – men only existed for her personal gratification. She was sexy and she knew it.

Sylvanha may have lacked the contacts, directional-sense and detailed knowledge of an experienced guide, but she was terrific fun and gave us a fascinating insight into 'her' Rio. Within hours of meeting her and still suffering with jet lag, photographer Anton and I found ourselves in a Samba club with Sylvanha and several of her (equally sexy) friends. We left, drunk and exhausted at 4am, but she stayed until six.

Her carefree spirit was indicative of her wealthy upbringing, but she was not oblivious to Brazil's social problems. Our encounter with Joao Henrisue, a 14 year-old boy from a favela who wanted to be a doctor, brought tears to her eyes as she decried the lack of social mobility.

On paper, Brazil is a wealthy country, but its ladder of opportunity has several rungs missing and those at the bottom often find it impossible to make the leap. In a country renowned for its flair and hedonistic spirit, they live a life filled with poverty and fear. Our guide had been born lucky, and she knew it.

ESCADARIA SELARON
RIO DE JANEIRO

Football and Catholicism remain central to the Brazilian way of life

"That's the one, that's the one," exclaims Silvinha, pointing feverishly at a youthful policeman in Rio de Janeiro. The young officer, it's quickly revealed, had had the audacity to stop our guide while she'd been driving whilst high on cannabis.

'I told him I just wanted to get home,' she said. 'I had to pay him BRL20 [Brazilian Reals, about £5] just to get rid of him. He was being ridiculous – everybody in Rio drives when they're stoned or drunk.'

It's an unusual introduction to life in Rio. This southern hemisphere city of 13 million people, nestling on the Atlantic coast is not the economic powerhouse of Brazil – that honour belongs to Sao Paulo – but it is its cultural and spiritual heartbeat. When most people are asked to bring to mind Brazil, they think of Copacabana, street carnivals and caparinhas. In other words, they think of Rio.

Most men also tend to think of beautiful, bronzed lovelies, dressed in the skimpiest of thong bikinis.

'In Rio, you go to the beach nearly every day,' says Silvinha, 'so fitness is really important – you have to look good.' It's a tantalising thought, but this is an overcast, autumnal day and the temperature is a mere 25 degrees. The goddesses are staying away and the beach is all but empty.

'Cariocas [Rio residents] won't go to the beach if the sun isn't out,' Silvinha informs me.

Denied an afternoon's ogling, we decide to undertake some reconnaissance work in our Discovery. This wasn't our original choice of transport; we were supposed to be driving a Range Rover Sport, which seemed more in tune with Rio's brash, ostentatious image. But in the week before our arrival, the solitary LR press car was crashed by an over-eager local, and we're in a Discovery V8 HSE.

Brazil's economic inequality is well-documented and a Land Rover remains a relatively rare sight in these parts, with just 323 sold in the whole of Brazil last year. This car's styling might be deliberately utilitarian, but it's still a potent symbol of affluence. Car-jacking is not exactly uncommon in Rio, which makes me feel slightly uneasy.

'At night, you shouldn't stop at a red light,' says Silvinha. 'It's safer to keep going – even the police agree.' She's wary and streetwise, but anxious to defend her home town. This pretty, affluent 25 year-old has, she assures us, never been mugged.

We cruise the coastline. Rio is famous for having 37 beaches, but I'm astonished to discover that the best-known, Copacabana – which is littered with beach volleyball and soccer nets – is actually man-made. The waves have a venomous

It's impossible not to get caught up in the Brazilian spirit, especially after a caipirinha or two

quality that I've witnessed in few other parts of the world. Further up the coast, the conditions for surfing are almost peerless.

While Copacabana sucks in the tourists, the adjacent beach at Ipanema is the most popular with locals, however. A series of numbered lifeguard posts define its geography and the post beside which you sit defines your social standing. When the sun is out, post nine is the place to be if you're uber-cool, but it's deserted today.

We park the Disco and take a stroll through Ipanema. Like most major cities, Rio is divided into different districts, each boasting its own character. Ipanema is self-consciously wealthy and the street of Garcia D'Avila boasts luxury goods shops that could be found anywhere in the world. The people populating its cafés and pavements could have been plucked from Milan or Monte Carlo. Little wonder that Antonio Carlos Jobim sang of *The Girl from Ipanema* that she would "look straight ahead, not at me" – they really do pass over anyone less well-dressed.

Returning to the Land Rover, we plot a route back to the hotel. The driving standards in Rio seem surprisingly good. There are some erratic manoeuvres, but little of the aggression associated with most European cities. Perversely, one suspects that the city's threatening reputation makes people less likely to beep their horns and hurl abuse at other road users. And the sheer size of the Discovery is a definite bonus.

It's Saturday night, which in Rio, is party time. The district of Lapa reverberates to the sound of samba, but it doesn't kick into life until after midnight. For a travel-weary Brit, this sounds like a chore, but after couple of caipirinhas I'm buzzing with anticipation. The caipirinha is Brazil's unofficial drink and consists of cachaça (a high proof cane spirit), lime, sugar and crushed ice. It sounds simple, but the best ones are beautifully executed.

By 1am, I find myself in a laid-back samba club in the heart of the Lapa district. Music is central to the Brazilian way of life and sexy, toned and tanned bodies gyrate around me, moving easily to the rhythm. Pale, flabby, musically inept and unnecessarily tall, I find myself feeling distinctly self-conscious. Time for another caipirinha.

Next morning, the sun has still not got his hat on and so we decide to make our way up to what is arguably Rio's most famous landmark: Cristo Redentor or Christ the Redeemer. This 38m high statue of Christ sits on top of the 710m high Corcovado Mountain and to get there, we must wind our way out of the city.

Mid-way up the mountain, we lose our way and call upon the services of 14 year-old Joao Henrisue. With a handful of contemporaries, he waits by the roadside in an official T-shirt, hoping that tourists will lose their way and seek his assistance. For BRL10 (about £2.50), he will give them a guided tour of the Christ.

LAND ROVER
BA-CAMACARI
JQH-7610

LAND ROVER
JQH·7610

'... the city has seen better days, but it still possesses an indefatigable spirit.'

Joao's work is sporadic and there is no guaranteed income, but what little money he earns must support his mother and his three siblings. According to statistics, 22 per cent of Brazilians live in poverty and, in Rio's giant favelas, the drug barons are the law.

'It is dangerous in the favela and I know lots of people who've died because of drugs,' he tells us. 'I study at night for a better future. I want to be a doctor.'

He smiles optimistically, poses for the camera and begins the wait for the next tourist who may or may not need his help.

Our guide, born into happier circumstances, is emotional. 'He will not be a doctor,' she says; 'There are no opportunities for him. This is the problem with my country.'

It's impossible to travel through Rio without seeing a favela. These vast, ramshackle communities sprawl across the hillsides and, more often than not, sit side-by-side with expensive condominiums. Some companies run guided tours of the largest, Rocinha favela, but such ghoulish voyeurism is not to my taste.

We arrive at the Christ to find it shrouded in cloud, so quickly make our way to Santa Teresa.

Sitting on a hillside overlooking the city, Santa Teresa's colonial-style architecture is a throwback to Brazil's Portuguese past. There is even a quaint bonde (tram), which links the area with the centre of Rio. It's here that we stumble across Jambeirio, a young artist who's painting a mural depicting South America's footballing greats. Cafu and Deco from the contemporary team stand beside the troubled Argentinean genius of yesteryear, Diego Maradona, dressed in a shirt that's half-Brazilian and half-Argentinian.

Football is still an all-consuming passion for Brazilians, both rich and poor. For decades, the flamboyant success of the national team has been a wonderful antidote to the problems at home.

The local teams are no less keenly supported and on this Sunday evening, we make our way to the Maracana Stadium, which hosted the World Cup Final in 1950. We leave the Discovery in a multi-storey car park and take a taxi to the Maracana. An unofficial world record crowd of 199,854 turned up in 1950 to watch Brazil lose the World Cup Final 1-2 to neighbours Uruguay. Fifty years on, the stadium is being renovated and there are maybe only 30,000 here to watch a local derby between Flamengo and Botafogo.

I've been to hundreds of live football games in the UK, but only the FA Cup final can compare with the atmosphere in the Maracana tonight. There is a huge swell of emotion and a mass outpouring of passion that seems to transcend the football. I spend more time watching the crowd than the action on the pitch.

In many ways, the Maracana is rather like Rio as a whole: the city has seen better days, but it still possesses an indefatigable spirit.

First published on the 4car website, 9th June 2006

The Best 4x4 x Land Rio

SENNA TEN YEARS ON

Visiting Sao Paulo on the tenth anniversary of Aryton Senna's death

Photographs ANTON WATTS

I was sixteen years old when Ayrton Senna was killed in the San Marino Grand Prix at Imola. An apparently innocuous accident ended the life of a racing legend and his death had a significant effect on me.

I never met Senna, but he was as close to a hero as I ever had. Effortlessly charismatic both in and out of the car, he embodied everything that was cool about motor racing. He was flamboyant, edgy, apparently fearless and utterly determined to win. These were all qualities that appealed to an impressionable adolescent.

But for the people of Brazil, Senna was much more than a racing idol. At a time of considerable national hardship, he was a source of hope and inspiration. It mattered not that he was a rich kid from the posh side of town – when he raced, he raced for Brazil. His famous yellow and green helmet was a statement of patriotic intent that was instantly recognisable across the globe.

Senna's death had an enduring legacy. The Grand Prix community introduced a raft of changes to improve driver protection and, to date, there have been no more fatalities in Formula One. In Brazil, the Senna Foundation continues to improve the lives of the country's less privileged.

For the tenth anniversary of his death – May 1st 2004 – I travelled to Senna's home city of Sao Paulo to learn a little more about the man and his legacy. It was to prove a fascinating and immensely rewarding journey, but it was a difficult story to write.

Normally as a journalist you try and take a dispassionate view of the subject, to remain once removed. But in Sao Paulo I got caught up in the emotion of the moment. When Senna's old karting mechanic started to break down during our interview, I wanted to cry too.

To facilitate the trip, I had turned to Honda for help. Honda engines had powered Senna to three World Championships and the Japanese company had a huge presence in Brazil. The local Honda officials kindly helped with some of the logistics and provided us with a driver and a translator. Our car – a Honda Accord – was bullet-proof, and photographer Anton and I travelled in the back.

For the first two days, we went everywhere with the windows up and the air-con on. But as we entered the favela (shanty town), the driver lowered the front windows. "Err, what's going on?" we asked. It was quickly explained that this was the Brazilian equivalent of the British salute. You are saying, 'I am not armed and I am not a threat'.

"At night, you should turn off the headlights and turn on the interior light so that everyone can see who you are," said our translator. "Someone forgot recently and they were shot to death." We were also warned that there had recently been a drug killing in the favela and tensions were running high.

It was a graphic reminder that, ten years after Senna's death, Brazil's problems are far from over.

BOSS
MENS FASHION

Visiting an orphanage in the Paraiso Polis Favela (above); and the Senna Foundation (below)

Maria José Clemente raises a finger and points at a poster on the orphanage wall. It features Ayrton Senna in white overalls emblazoned with a red 'S' and was probably taken in late 1993, just before his ill-fated move to Williams. "All my material happiness, I owe to Ayrton," she says. "Every time that I am in difficulty, I hold a figure of Ayrton and pray for his help. And every time, he comes to my aid."

Spoken in earnest and impassioned Portugese, it sounds to an outsider like the obsessive mutterings of a celebrity stalker. Until you find out just why Clemente feels so close to the racing legend. She first met Senna 15 years ago when he came to visit her orphanage in São Paulo's Paraiso Polis Favela.

"He visited here several times," she explains, "because he was worried about the future of the Brazilian children." She points to a chair on which he sat, and talks of a helmet he gave her as a gift. "We have a small replica for the children," she says. "But it would be too risky to keep the original here."

The arrival of a Formula One world champion in the favela must have been some occasion. The Paraiso Polis is the largest of several favelas in São Paulo and is home to 70,000 people, who live in its heaving mass of brick-built shacks. It's a world in which drugs are the dominant force. Just two days ago, a young man was shot dead in a drugs-related murder, and I've been warned that the atmosphere is tense.

I take the precaution of turning up in a bulletproof Honda Accord, but fortunately, my immediate safety is guaranteed by my association with Clemente and her orphanage.

Clemente has an immediate standing among her peers, thanks in part to her long-standing association with Senna. She's seen as something like a mortal receiving a saint. But it's unlikely Ayrton saw it that way, and it quickly becomes clear he must have respected and admired Clemente and her work a great deal.

"I was looking after about 300 children," she explains. "And at the end of every month, a food truck started arriving, containing enough supplies to feed us all. I also became the first person from the favela to receive free medical treatment from a private hospital. Nobody would tell me who was paying for it, but after he died, I found out that it was Ayrton."

Today, the Ayrton Senna Foundation (set up after his death) continues to send food trucks to the Escolina Lar Casa Humilde, the children's home, and when the diabetic Clemente had her right leg amputated three months ago, the foundation picked up the bill. "Gerhard Berger is a friend of the surgeon," she continues, "and now Gerhard is having a prosthetic limb made for me in Rome." It's the sort of story that would sound utterly ludicrous, if it wasn't true.

Like so many other F1 fans, I can recall in intricate detail Senna's first lap of the 1993 European Grand Prix at Donington Park or his Monaco victories. But in Brazil, his legacy runs much deeper, which is something that Maria José Clemente epitomises. Here, in the poor, smog-ridden suburbs of São Paulo, the Senna legend has transcended the man. And this is what I came to explore.

Sid Mosca is someone who knows all about the potency of the Senna legend. This year, he expects to sell around 300 replicas of Senna's famous crash helmet at about £500 each. It might seem cynical to you or me, but the man has earned the right to do so. It was Sid Mosca, after all, who designed Senna's unmistakable yellow and green headwear.

It takes a while to locate his glass-fronted showroom, tucked between hotels that offer rooms by the hour. On arriving, I'm confronted by an elaborate array of racing cars, but it's the helmets that really catch the eye. There must be 30 or more, arranged in glass cabinets and most are instantly recognisable. Piquet, Michael Andretti, Hakkinen, Barrichello, Massa and Zonta are all represented, and so, of course, is the yellow and green of Ayrton Senna.

Mosca must be in his late fifties and is dressed in a simple black polo shirt and

Tche taught Senna how to race karts; the famous yellow helmet

sandy chinos. His handshake is firm and he leads me up to his office. "I developed the design for him before he entered his first kart world championship in 1978," Mosca begins. "Even then, he wanted to take Brazil to the world. When I watched Senna race, I always had a strong feeling, because I was the creator of the face."

In his office there is an original helmet, from the Lotus-Honda era, which Senna gave him – even the intercom system is still in place. He talks about how he and Ayrton used to fly model planes, and how they rode motorbikes together.

"His greatest love in life was to drive, but he always wanted to make other people happy. When he lifted the flag, he was saying 'always forward Brazil'. Maybe one day he will be remembered not just as a great driver, but also as a great patriot."

When we leave Mosca, we make a short journey to a tiny workshop beside the Interlagos GP circuit. At first glance, it appears that the entrance is covered in graffiti, but a closer look reveals a deliberate motif bearing the name 'Tche.' A small old man wanders out to greet our arrival. He is dressed in a short-sleeve blue jacket and looks like a school janitor, but Tche, the Spanish engineer, is crucial to the Senna story. While Mosca's helmet design helped create the image, Tche worked on the man.

He leads the way through a dimly lit workshop that must contain more than 50 kart engines. Arriving outside his office, a sign in English reads 'Senna Forever.' Below it is a freehand drawing of Senna in a Tche-prepared kart. Inside, the office walls are a collage of racing images from the past three decades. There are more photographs of the young Senna, and a host of other drivers, including one of the current favourite among Latin American drivers, Juan Pablo Montoya.

"I worked with Senna from 1974 until 1981, when he moved to Europe," says Tche. "We got on well and his father did not interfere with the relationship between us, which was very important. Ayrton was always asking questions and always obedient. Every driver needs the right instructor and, in that sense, I created Senna."

Somewhat contentiously, Tche doesn't actually believe that Ayrton was truly exceptional. "He was not really special, but he always followed all the right steps. I could see that he wanted to be a winner, and I showed him how to be a winner. He became a polished diamond."

In the workshop, Tche shows me one of Senna's earliest kart engines. While most of the rivals prepared their engines themselves under Tche's supervision, Tche personally engineered all of Senna's engines, which helped create an air of invincibility. Even then, Senna was playing the psychological card to full advantage.

He shows me a letter, handwritten to 'meu grande amigo Tche' and signed 'Abracos Ayrton.' The letter is dated 16th September, 1979, when Senna was in Milan, preparing for the kart world championships. It's a fascinating document and reveals so many of the personality traits that Senna would later exhibit in Formula One, including his warmth and compassion: 'Who really put me on the right path? Who taught me everything I know? Who is here in everything? The person who helped me arrive where I am and who is responsible for my glories is you.'

But there are also signs of the petty jealousies and feuding that would come to blight his grand prix career. He complains that the English are jealous of him, and expresses his concern about an English driver, Terry Fullerton: 'the Englishman is dead jealous, but that's fine with me,' he writes.

Tche acknowledges that jealousy was central to the Senna enigma. "He was always jealous of Prost, who was always a gentleman to him," he says. "I criticised him after Suzuka in 1990 (when Senna barged Prost off the road to claim the championship), because it was not the right thing to do. But Ayrton had been disappointed when Ferrari chose Prost instead of him."

The two men remained close throughout Senna's life and last spoke before the 1994 Brazilian Grand Prix. "I asked him if he was OK," he says, "and he said 'Yes, but I miss you.' He said the Williams was like a pig to drive and he was being bruised and battered. I could feel something was wrong and I stopped asking questions because he was becoming stressed."

Sid Mosca was the man who designed and painted Senna's helmet

Tche with a kart engine from Senna's early career; graveside tributes

A month later Tche's friend was dead and the recollection of that day brings tears to the old man's eyes. "Life will never be the same again," he says. "Never."

Next morning dawns with the calendar reading May 1. It's 10 years to the day since Senna lost control of his Williams in the Tamburello corner at Imola and, moments later, lost his life.

Senna's grave is located in Morumbi cemetery, south-east of the city centre. It's a little after 9am when we arrive and a number of people are already there. Situated underneath a tree, the memorial to Senna constitutes no more than a plaque placed in the ground, bearing the words, 'Nada Pode me separar do amor de dues', which translates as 'Nobody can separate me from the love of God.'

It ought to be a moment for some quiet contemplation, but it's disturbed by the presence of a bizarre figure dressed in a faux racing suit handing out fliers for a Senna fan club. He's even called his son Ayrton Senna and the pair are posing for photographs next to the plaque. Few seem to be concerned that they are trampling on the grave of two-year-old Marcelo de Aravid Contier, who lies next to Senna.

At the exit to the cemetery, we're met by souvenir sellers who are trying to cash in on the occasion. Such exploitation, though excusable to some extent, given the poverty of some people here, is of deep concern to the custodians of the Ayrton Senna Foundation.

The Foundation was established to promote the welfare of Brazilian children. It's located on the 15th floor of a high-rise building in the heart of São Paulo. The furniture is expensive and the pastel ambience could have been plucked from any trendy western bar, but the foundation's appearance belies its philanthropic mission.

Launched in November 1994, the ASF is a non-profit making, non-governmental organisation committed to ensuring that Brazil's youth fulfil their potential. Last year, it invested over £3.5 million in social projects that, in 2004, should reach 1.25 million children.

"The foundation grew out of a conversation Ayrton had with his sister Viviane shortly before he died," explains Margareth Goldenberg, who carries the somewhat grandiose title of Superintendent. "He spoke very clearly about the need to establish an organisation that could help the people of Brazil. The Foundation is the 'concretization' of the dream of Ayrton Senna." She continues, "Ayrton has a magical connection with the Brazilian people. He was the brother, the son, or the boyfriend of everybody in Brazil. His appeal is mythical, it's not rational."

But why should the Brazilian public have such an affinity with Senna? Why not Nelson Piquet or Emerson Fittipaldi, both of whom were Brazilian world champions? "Ayrton came to represent the country at a time when it was very down," says Goldenberg. "There were governmental and economic problems, and the people's self-esteem was very low.

"Then, on a Sunday morning, they would wake up to see Senna putting Brazil on top of the world. He created a sense of magic inside the Brazilian people. They started to believe that if a Brazilian could win in such a technological arena, they could win at anything. Ayrton was not just a sportsman winning a game."

Goldenberg has work to do and I make my way to the Universidade de São Paulo, which plays home to the Projeto Esporte Talento. One of 13 similar projects supported by the Senna Foundation, it seeks to facilitate human development through the medium of sport. Underprivileged or underachieving children are selected from local schools to attend a four-day course. Marcos Vinicus Movra E Silva is one of the project's coordinators: "We concentrate on teaching Senna's core values – morality, hard work and focus," he explains. "The idea is to increase the children's confidence. The school drop-out rate for those involved in the course has fallen from 40 to just 2 per cent."

I'm introduced to a young man who is wearing a T-shirt depicting 'Senninha', the cartoon character launched by Senna in early '94. His name is Fulina and he's 14 years-old.

ESCOLINHA LAR

"Before I came here, I would stay at home, be on the streets and be naughty," he explains. "There are a lot of drugs where I live and I know lots of bad people. Now I can learn things and pass them on to my friends."

Fulina is too young to remember Senna the driver and it seems strange to hear him talk of this man with an almost religious zeal. "I only remember a day when my mother cried," he admits. "I was told that there had been a terrible accident."

I return to the favela for a final time before catching the flight home. It's lunchtime and I'm invited onto the roof of a house for an impromptu barbecue. As I sup a beer, munch on red meat and watch the children dance around me, I'm afforded the opportunity to reflect on what has been an extraordinary visit.

Brazil is a country where tremendous wealth sits just across the street from desperate poverty. And while Senna may have grown up in a well off family, away from the favelas, there's no sense of bitterness among those from this less fortunate background.

Instead, the population has apotheosised Senna for his achievements, to regard him – ironically, given how exceptional he was – as a sort of Everyman figure. This is a man who, even at the height of his battles with Prost for the Formula One world championship, still found time to visit an orphanage in a downtrodden part of town. Back then, he represented a beacon of hope for a depressed population. He still does, through the work of the foundation established by his sister, and given such a pervasive influence even after his death, it's little wonder that Senna's image is shown a deference normally only reserved for religious figures.

But there's something else too. Ayrton Senna was not only a winner, but a quintessentially Brazilian winner. He appeared to race with that insouciance and flair that encapsulates the spirit of the people. Like the great Brazilian football teams of the Seventies, Senna's style was carnival style, as much a celebration of a sport as a competition within it.

It's perhaps this quality, more than any other, that ensures Senna's saintly status a decade after his untimely death.

First printed in *Top Gear* magazine, July 2004

THE PHOTOGRAPHERS

LEE BRIMBLE

Lee Brimble has only been shooting cars for the past four years, but has quickly established an impressive reputation. After learning his craft working as a photographic assistant, Lee cut his editorial teeth as the staff photographer at *Zero* magazine before turning freelance. He now works for some of the world's leading automotive titles, and is one of the key photographic contributors to the UK's biggest-selling car magazine, *Top Gear*. Lee's distinctive style has also caught the eye of commercial clients, including Mercedes-Benz, Nissan and the supercar club, écurie25.

www.leebrimble.co.uk

CHARLIE MAGEE

As one of the UK's leading automotive photographers, Charlie Magee has photographed subjects as diverse as the Bugatti Atlantic, all the way through to the latest hydrogen and electric sports cars. His commissions are primarily from British magazines, including *Autocar, Car Magazine* and the like, but his work can also been seen in international publications, including many North American titles. Editorial tasks take Charlie all over the world – one week will see him shivering in temperatures of minus 20 degrees in a frozen desert with a Jeep in Greenland, while the next he's chasing a FedEx plane from New York to Miami in a Bentley GTC. But to all of these challenges, Charlie brings his own inimitable style of energy and excitement.

www.charliemagee.com

IAN DAWSON

Ian Dawson has been a successful freelance photographer since the 1970s. To have made a living through the lens of his beloved cameras, to have felt the thrill of having his work published, and the excitement of sharing his point of vision are for him privileges which have never faded. Ian has travelled widely and worked for most of the world's finest automotive titles, while striving always to look afresh at everything around him. His photography is influenced by his early study of sculpture and painting, and his constant endeavour to find new terms of expression has earned him many admirers from among his peers.

STAN PAPIOR

Stan Papior is an award-winning photographer whose work has been published for the past 20 years in some of the world's most respected car magazines. But it is in his day job, as the chief photographer of *Autocar*, the oldest car magazine in the world, that he is best known to British fans of cars and photography. Over the years Stan has played an instrumental role in ensuring that *Autocar*, with its punishing weekly schedule, maintains standards of photographic excellence that remain the envy of even the best monthly motoring titles.

www.stanpapior.com

TOM SALT

Tom Salt is a freelance photographer born in New York, educated in England but now living near Lubeck in Germany. Working primarily for editorial and corporate clients including the BBC, *The Times,* United Airlines and the *Financial Times*, Tom travels all over the world. Recent assignments have taken him to Canada, Dubai, and Pripyat, the workers' city abandoned after the explosion of the Chernobyl nuclear power station in 1986. Tom also works on his own projects, documenting the remains of the former East/West German border, and photographing the ruins of defensive structures constructed during the Second World War.

www.tomsalt.com

ANTON WATTS

Australian born Anton Watts has developed an enviable reputation as one of the world's leading automotive photographers. After leaving his homeland for the UK in the early 1990s, Anton made his reputation at *Car Magazine*, where his fresh, instinctive approach complemented the magazine's step-ahead style. Now freelance, Anton is a regular contributor to editorial magazines including *Top Gear*, as well as photographing advertising campaigns for automotive clients such as Mercedes, Volkswagen and Jaguar. Anton is now based in Los Angeles, but works throughout the world.

www.antonwatts.com

WALDO VAN DER WAAL

South African born and bred, Waldo van der Waal has photographed some typically South African things, such as wild animals and crime scenes, but his love of cars has always come first. Waldo has worked on six continents, rolled down a Bolivian mountainside in a Range Rover, and dived with sharks, but the African thunderstorms always call him home. Even though he is mercenary enough to go wherever the job dictates, Waldo is happiest photographing the country of his birth – as long as there's a car somewhere in the frame.

PEKING TO PARIS
– THE ULTIMATE DRIVING ADVENTURE

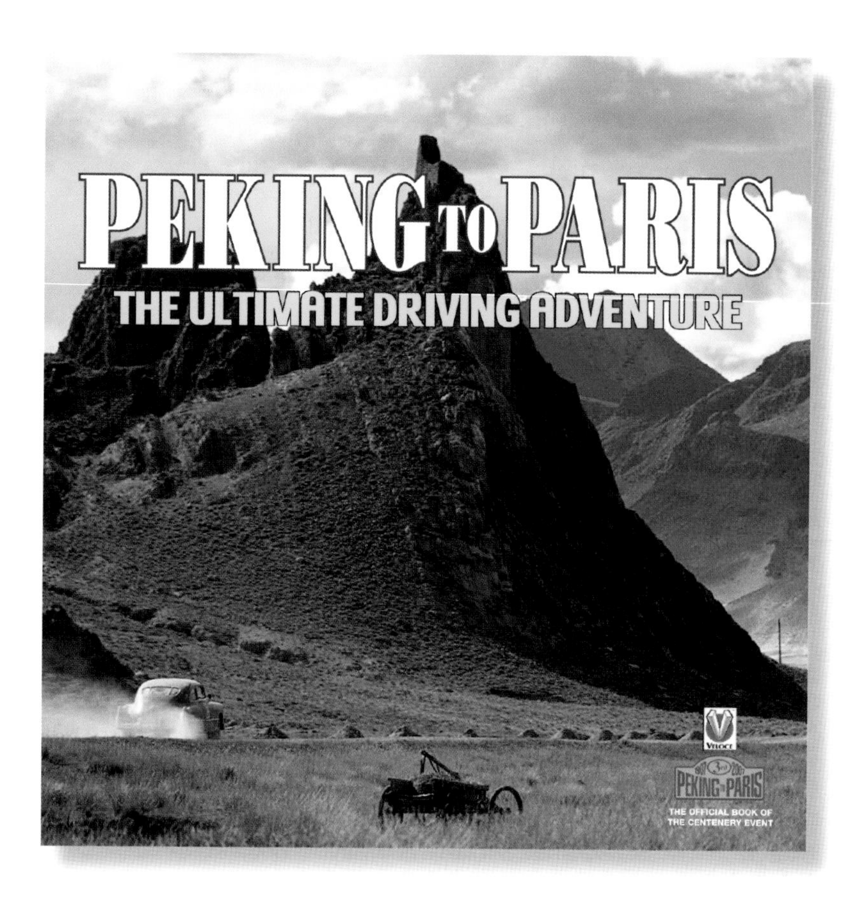

Hardback • 25x25cm • £29.99* UK/$59.95* US • 224 pages • Over 200 illustrations • www.velocebooks.com
ISBN: 978-1-84584-120-1

Man and machine against the elements, driving where no car has gone before. That was the impossible challenge of 1907, when a handful of buccaneering, madcap motorists took up the idea of a Paris newspaper - to prove that the car could now go anywhere - by driving the longest distance between two capital cities: from Peking to Paris. To mark the 100th anniversary of the original 'Great Race', over 100 cars set out to drive the route of Prince Borghese in 2007.

In everything from authentic veteran Italas, to vintage Bentleys and classic Aston Martins, drivers from 26 nationalities came together to pit their wits and their cars by driving 40 days from the Great Wall of China, across the Gobi Desert, through ten days of wilderness crossing Monglia's vast plains, to Russia ... and on to Moscow's Red Square, St Petersburg, Estonia, Latvia, Poland, Germany; the survivors finally rolling into Paris for an amazing party.

This is the inside story of a great driving adventure and the human endeavour needed to complete an amazing route. The Official Book of the Peking to Paris also covers the original event, including previously unpublished photographs.

Exactly 100 years on from the original achievement, rally enthusiasts discovered that poor fuel, food and water, and finding their way to distant horizons remain the same challenges as faced by the original pioneers.

** Prices subject to change.*

MOTOR MOVIES

– THE POSTERS!

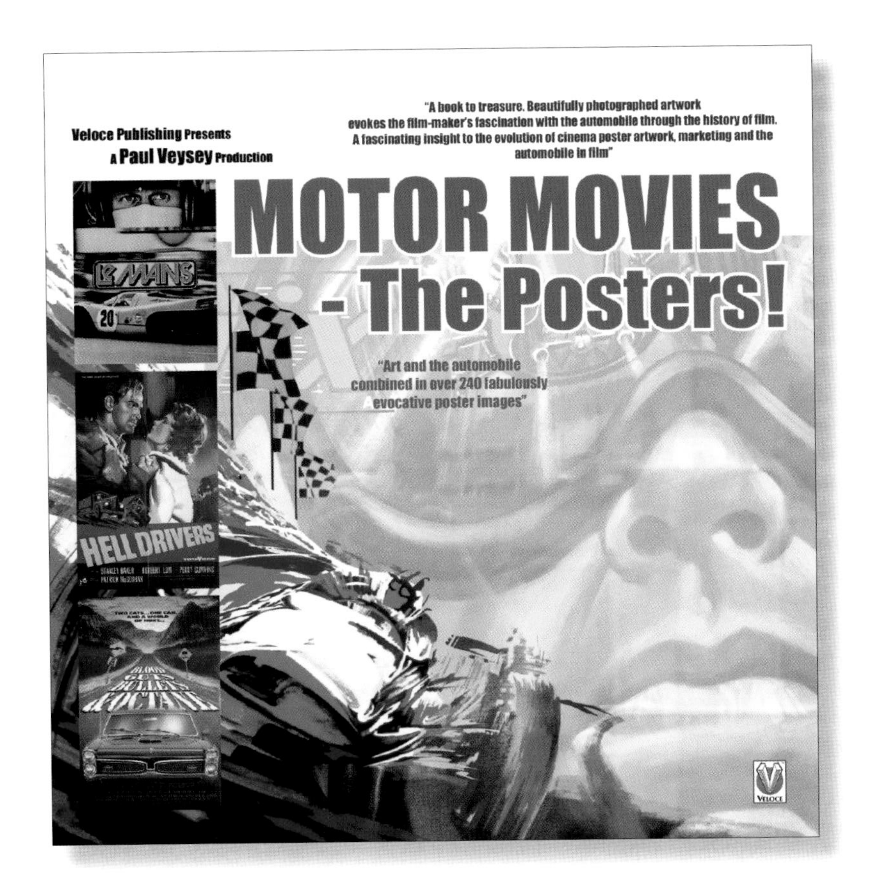

Hardback • 25x25cm • £34.99 • 224 pages • 250 original colour photographs • www.velocebooks.com

ISBN: 978-1-84584-127-0

From the late 19th century the progress of the movies has paralleled that of the motorcar. Now, for the first time, these developments are chronicled through the medium of the movie poster. This book celebrates the progression from the simple and crude, through the functional, the ambitious and the barking mad, right up to today's high-tech, computer generated, but often soulless examples of poster art. By presenting poster chronologically, the book takes you on a journey through the 20th century in black and white, sepia, hand colouring, stone-litho, and glorious technicolour; and shows the obsessively accurate, the artist's impression, the photographic and wildly imaginative depictions of the automobile. The development of product placement in marketing is also well illustrated. Why did the Mustang appear in so little publicity for *Bullitt?* Where was the Mini in most of the world's publicity for *The Italian Job?* Why wasn't the Alfa Romeo Dueto prominent in the advertising of *The Graduate?*

The book doesn't provide intricate plot lines or vast cast lists. instead, it shows how different countries promoted the same movie, and gives a brief guide to buying posters. Beautifully photographed artwork is guaranteed to bring back memories of favourite cars in movies and give a fascinating insight to the evolution of cinema, marketing and the automobile. With 250 pictures of rare originals and a star rating system for rarity, this is a beautiful book to browse, and a valuable investment guide.

** Prices subject to change.*

Index

THE LITTLE BOOK OF SMART

What started off as an idea from Swiss watchmaker Swatch eventually evolved into the successful launch of the smart brand, now an integral part of the Mercedes-Benz family, which in its first ten years, achieved sales of more than three quarters of a million cars around the world.

Well publicised financial woes, the launch of at least one inappropriate model range, and the subsequent rationalisation of the entire product line-up meant plenty of problems along the way.

These days, the future looks rosier. An all-new fortwo model range was launched in 2007, along with the announcement of the long-awaited debut of the smart brand in the American market for 2008. The latest model is more sophisticated and more in tune with today's buyers' tastes, though losing none of the inventiveness, practicality and sheer chic appeal of its predecessors.

In *the little book of smart*, author and smart fanatic Paul Jackson guides us through the entire history of the brand, its highs and lows, its successes and failures, and on to today – with the very latest fortwo line-up promising major sales worldwide and, of course, helping to pave the way for a future for smart in the USA. It's a fascinating tale, told succinctly and in an entertaining style, and complemented by full colour photography throughout.

Just like the cars, the little book of smart is both compact and stylish.